RAFFAELE MATTIOLI LECTURES

In honour of the memory of Raffaele Mattioli, who was for many years its manager and chairman, Banca Commerciale Italiana has established the Mattioli Fund as a testimony to the continuing survival and influence of his deep interest in economics, the humanities and sciences.

As its first enterprise the Fund has established a series of annual lectures on the history of economic thought, to be called the Raffaele Mattioli Lectures.

In view of the long association between the Università Commerciale Luigi Bocconi and Raffaele Mattioli, who was an active scholar, adviser and member of the governing body of the University, it was decided that the lectures in honour of his memory should be delivered at the University, which together with Banca Commerciale Italiana, has undertaken the task of organising them.

Distinguished academics of all nationalities, researchers and others concerned with economic problems will be invited to take part in this enterprise, in the hope of linking pure historical research with a debate on economic theory and practical policy.

In creating a memorial to the cultural legacy left by Raffaele Mattioli, it is hoped above all that these lectures and the debates to which they give rise will prove a fruitful inspiration and starting point for the development of a tradition of research and academic studies like that already long established in other countries, and that this tradition will flourish thanks to the new partnership between the Università Commerciale Luigi Bocconi and Banca Commerciale Italiana.

INSTITUTIONAL ECONOMICS
REVISITED

RAFFAELE MATTIOLI FOUNDATION

Shigeto Tsuru

*INSTITUTIONAL ECONOMICS
REVISITED*

CAMBRIDGE
UNIVERSITY PRESS

Published by the Press Syndicate of the University of Cambridge
The Pitt Building, Trumpington Street, Cambridge CB2 1RP
40 West 20th Street, New York, NY 10011-4211, USA
10 Stamford Road, Oakleigh, Victoria, 3166, Australia

Edited by Carlo Secchi, assisted by Cynthia Panas-Avesani

HB
99.5
T78
1993

© Shigeto Tsuru, 1993, Exclusive licensee 1993-1996
Banca Commerciale Italiana, Milano, Italy

First published 1993

Printed in Italy

Library of Congress Cataloging in Publication Data
Main entry under title:
Institutional Economics Revisited
(Raffaele Mattioli Lectures)
At head of title: Raffaele Mattioli Foundation.
Bibliography.

1. Institutional Economics
2. Economic History

I. Tsuru, Shigeto. II. Raffaele Mattioli Foundation. III. Series.

HB 3732.D43   1984   338.9   84-21366

British Library Cataloguing in Publication Data
Tsuru, Shigeto
Institutional Economics Revisited
(Raffaele Mattioli Lectures)
1. Economics
I. Title II. Series
339 HB 172.5
ISBN 0 521 440 21 1

FLORIDA STATE
UNIVERSITY LIBRARIES

NOV 18 1993

TALLAHASSEE, FLORIDA

CONTENTS

CONTENTS

PREFACE

The reason I propose to 'revisit' institutional economics is that in the condition of disarray[1] which the discipline of economics finds itself today I feel that institutionalism needs to be reappraised as a school of thought with promises of greater relevance to the task which our profession is called upon to wrestle with today.

The term 'institutionalism' has been applied in the past to a doctrinal movement in the United States from about 1890 when Thorstein Veblen began his academic career at Cornell University; and he, along with John Commons and Wesley Mitchell, have been regarded as the main protagonists of this school.

However, orthodox judgment on this movement, as exemplified by the standard textbook of Paul Samuelson, is that '40 years ago Institutionalism seemed to wither away as an effective counterforce in economics'.[2] Kenneth E. Boulding, too, who has certainly broadened the vista of our discipline into sociological and even natural-scientific dimensions, had an occasion to describe institutional economics as an 'interlude nevertheless which ended for all practical purposes in the 1930s'.[3]

1. Cf. GUY ROUTH and PETER WILES, eds., *Economics in Disarray*, Oxford: Blackwell, 1984.
2. PAUL A. SAMUELSON, *Economics*, 11th edition, Tokyo: MacGraw-Hill Kogakusha, 1979. In the 12th edition of this texbook (1985), co-authored by William D. Nordhaus, the reference to institutionalism itself was omitted.
3. KENNETH E. BOULDING, 'A New Look at Institutionalism', *American Economic Review*, May 1957, p. 1.

I beg to differ in this judgment and I shall try to explain why in the course of my series of lectures on this occasion.

I begin with a quotation from Allan Gruchy who rather recently characterized 'institutionalists' as those who 'inquired into problems such as the impact of technological change on the structure and functioning of the economic system, the power relations among economic interest groups, the logic of the process of industrialization, and the determination of national goals and priorities'.[1]

If this is the proper definition of 'institutionalism', I would say that the best hope for the revitalizing of economic science today lies in pursuing our inquiry in the direction Gruchy suggests; in particular, in focusing upon 'the impact of technological change on the structure and functioning of the economic system – which, incidentally, is none other than what Marx had in mind when he spoke of the dialectic relation of productive powers and the mode of production'.

This is why I begin this series of lectures with Karl Marx.

1. ALLAN G. GRUCHY, 'Institutional Economics: Its Development and Prospects', in ROLF STEPPACHER, BRIGITTE ZOGG-WALS and HERMAN HATZFELDT, *Economics in Institutional Perspective: Memorial Essays in Honor of William Kapp*, Lexington, Mass.: Lexington Books D. C. Heath and Co., 1977, p. 11.

SHIGETO TSURU

INSTITUTIONAL ECONOMICS
REVISITED

The *Raffaele Mattioli Lectures* were delivered by Shigeto Tsuru at the Università Commerciale Luigi Bocconi in Milano, from 20th to 22nd May 1985.

CHAPTER ONE

Reappraisal of Marxian Political Economy as 'Institutionalism' in the Broad Sense of the Term

Most characteristic of Marx's methodology in political economy is the emphasis on the importance of distinguishing between, and integrating, the *real* and the *value* aspects of the social production process. He wrote, for example:

> The labor process . . . is human action with a view to the production of use-values, appropriation of natural substances to human requirements; it is the necessary condition for effecting exchange of matter between man and Nature; it is the everlasting Nature-imposed condition of human existence, and therefore is independent of every social phase of the existence, or rather, is common to every such phase . . . As the taste of the porridge does not tell you who grew the oats, no more does this simple process tell you of itself what are the social conditions under which it is taking place, whether under the slave-owner's brutal lash, or the anxious eye of the capitalist, whether Cincinnatus carries it on in tilling his modest farm or a savage in killing wild animals with stones.[1]

Or again:[2]

> Every child knows that any nation which stopped work – I will not say for one year – but just for a couple of weeks, would die. And every child knows that the volume of products corresponding to the various needs calls for various and quantitatively determined amounts of total social labour. It is self-evident that this necessity of the division of social labour in certain proportions is not at all negated by the specific form of social production, but can only alter its mode of appearance. Natural laws can never be negated. Only the form in which those laws are applied can be altered in historically different situations. And the form in which this proportional division of labour asserts itself in a social situation and in which the connection of social labour

---

1. KARL MARX, *Capital*, vol. 1, Moscow: Foreign Language Publishing House, 1954-1962, pp. 183-184.

2. KARL MARX, Letter to Kugelmann, 11 July 1868, in *Letters on 'Capital'*, translated by ANDREW DRUMMOND, London: New Park Publications Ltd., 1983, p. 148.

asserts itself as a *private exchange* of the individual products of labour, is precisely the exchange-value of those products.

The *real* aspect is physical, transcending specific forms of socio-economic institutions, whereas the *value* aspect is social in the sense that it reflects an historically specific mode of production. Not only was Marx concerned with the distinction between the two aspects, but he was more eager to examine the interacting relations between the two, such as, for example, the impact of technological change (which is the physical aspect) upon the structure and functioning of the economic system (which is the social aspect) as well as the latter's influence upon the former. The famed thesis of historical materialism formulated as contradictions between productive *powers* and productive *relations* is intimately related to this methodology of his.

The progress of productive powers – the real aspect – may be likened to the rise in temperature of H_2O, while the specific institutional arrangement of productive relations – the value aspect – may be likened to the *forms* of H_2O, such as ice, water, and steam. And Marx's contention, in a word, was that, under capitalism, as productive powers make progress they are bound to have their *social*[1] character enhanced. This comes into conflict more and more with the private character of ownership of the means of production, and according to him this conflict will finally be resolved through 'bursting asunder of the capitalist integument'.[2]

However, just before this phrase, there appears one of the most revealing passages among Marx's writings detailing probable developments in the interaction between the real and value aspects under capitalism:

Hand in hand with this centralisation (of capital), or this expropriation of many capitalists by few, develop, on an ever-extending scale, the cooperative form of the labour-process, the conscious technical application of science, the methodical cultivation of the soil, the transformation of the instruments of labour into instruments of labour

1. 'Social' here means 'socially interrelated' or 'co-operative' form of labor process.
2. KARL MARX, *Capital*, vol. I, p. 763.

only usable in common, the economising of all means of production by their use as the means of production of combined, socialised labour, the entanglement of all peoples in the net of the world market, and with this, the international character of the capitalistic regime.[1]

This was written more than one hundred years ago and it is truly remarkable that the predictive insight revealed here has been to a large extent borne out. As Wassily Leontief wrote:

The record [of Marx's analysis of the long-run tendencies of the capitalist system] is indeed impressive: increasing concentration of wealth, rapid elimination of small and medium sized enterprise, progressive limitation of competition, incessant technological progress accompanied by the ever growing importance of fixed capital, and, last but not least, the undiminishing amplitude of recurrent business cycles – an unsurpassed series of prognostications fulfilled, against which modern economic theory with all its refinements has little to show indeed.

What significance has this list of successful anticipations for modern economic theory? Those who believe that Marx has said the last word on the subject invite us to quit. The attitude of other somewhat less optimistic – or should I say pessimistic – critics is well expressed by Professor Heimann: 'Marx's work remains by far the most comprehensive and impressive model of what we have to do.' The whole issue of the significance of Marxian economics for modern theory is thus transformed into a methodological question.[2]

What is still more remarkable is a longer-run prediction Marx made which postulated advances in the use of automation and which again bears on the interactive tension between the real and the value aspects. It reads as follows:

As large-scale industry advances, the creation of real wealth depends less on the labor time and the quantity of labor expended than on the power of the instrumentalities set in motion during the labor time. These instrumentalities, and their powerful effectiveness, are in no proportion to the immediate labor time which their production requires; their effectiveness rather depends on the attained level of science and technological progress; in other words, on the applica-

1. *Ibid.*, p. 763.
2. Wassily Leontief, 'The Significance of Marxian Economics for Present-Day Economic Theory', *American Economic Review*, Supplement, March 1938, p. 5.

tion of this science to production . . . Human labor then no longer appears as enclosed in the process of production – man rather relates himself to the process of production as supervisor and regulator . . . He stands outside of (*neben*) the process of production instead of being the principal agent in the process of production . . . In this transformation, the great pillar of production and wealth is no longer the immediate labor performed by man himself, nor his labor time, but the appropriation of his own universal productivity, i.e., his knowledge and his mastery of nature through his societal existence – in one word: the development of the societal individual . . . As soon as human labor, in its immediate form, has ceased to be the great source of wealth, labor time will cease, and must of necessity cease to be the measure of wealth, and the exchange value must of necessity cease to be the measure of use value . . . The mode of production which rests on the exchange value thus collapses.[1]

In Marx's mind was a thesis, as stated earlier, that the development of productive powers inevitably conditions the transformation of the mode of production; and it was his view that the condition for the atomistic attribution of labor's contribution to final products would inevitably disappear as automation and other forms of application of science to production progressed, and the 'societal individual' came to be developed. If the mode of production which rests on the exchange value thus comes to be undermined, it will be only natural that the determination of factor prices (the wage rate and the rate of interest) will lose the market objectivity of impersonal character and may become the product of power relations.

We may already be in such a stage in the evolving mode of production so that private firms (at least in the 'planning system' in the Galbraithian sense) can more or less determine the size of their mark-up ratio, and the organized workers, if strong enough, can successfully obtain their scheduled wage demands from their employers. To the extent factor prices are *administered* in such a way instead of being objectively determined in competitive markets, then what is expected of the 'invisible hand' is further

---

1. KARL MARX, *Grundisse der Kritik der Politischen Ökonomie*, Berlin: Dietz Verlag, 1953, pp. 592, 596, translated into English by HERBERT MARCUSE in his *öne Dimensional Man*, Routledge and Kegan Paul Ltd., London: 1964, pp. 35-36.

undermined. Not only is it the case that the market no longer serves as an impersonal arena through which consumers's sovereign decisions are faithfully conveyed to suppliers, but it must further be admitted that factor markets do not perform the function expected of them of objectively determining the rates at which factors are rewarded in proportion to their contribution to the total product. In fact, we may have come to a stage in our technical progress where it is becoming increasingly difficult to relate marginal input of a factor to incremental output.

The passage quoted above from Marx actually goes a step further by looking toward a stage in the evolution of the mode of production where 'labor time will cease, and must of necessity cease to be the measure of wealth, and the exchange value must of necessity cease to be the measure of use value'. In other words, society approaches the condition of 'a community of free individuals, carrying on their work with the means of production in common, in which the labor-power of all the different individuals is consciously applied as the combined labor-power of the community'.[1] There, the concept of 'income' will also radically change; and the principle of 'To each according to his needs!' will prevail.

In other words, according to Marx technological progress – the physical aspect – impinges upon the mode of production – the social aspect – in such a way that the latter undergoes qualitative changes often of major dimensions. In contrast to this is the neoclassical approach which has nurtured the tradition of explaining value relations, as far as possible, in terms of real categories, such as marginal utility of consumption goods and disutility of labor, etc.

Economists like Keynes and Harrod, who performed a pioneering role in the development of modern macroeconomic theory were, in their own way, aware of the peculiar difficulty which

---

1. *Ibid.*, p. 78; As a matter of fact, AFL-CIO, an American Trade Union Organization, in its published document, *Automation and Technological Change*, 1958, wrote: 'Automation in its largest sense means, in effect, the *end* of measurement of work . . . With automation, you can't measure output of a single man; you now have to measure simply equipment utilization. If that is generalization as a kind of concept . . . There is no longer, for example, any reason at all to pay a man by the piece or pay him by the hour'.

7

presented itself in the issue of the choice of units – the difficulty which stemmed from the double character (the value and the physical) of the production process, especially of the economic system as a whole. In criticizing Pigou's method of arriving at the net national dividend by deducting 'normal' obsolescence, Keynes made a revealing comment: 'Since this deduction is not a deduction in terms of money, he is involved in assuming that there can be a change in physical quantity, although there has been no physical change; i.e., he is covertly introducing changes in value'.[1] Keynes' solution was, as is well known, to adopt the labor-unit and/or the wage-unit. Harrod, too, wrestled with a similar problem when he posed the problem of whether neutral technical progress required new investment and answered that it was a question of definition – that the answer depended on whether a labor or goods standard of value is chosen. His preference was for the latter for a number of reasons which we shall not go into here.[2]

The distinction between a labor standard and a goods standard corresponds to that of the value aspect and the physical aspect respectively. Whereas microeconomics, for a capitalist society, can navigate almost entirely in the world of values, macroeconomics, especially of the dynamic type, finds it difficult to dissociate itself from the real or physical aspect of its subject matter. In this sense, the fact that Keynes, who was interested more in the shortrun problem with no technological change, chose a labor standard and Harrod, who was concerned with dynamic economics, chose a goods standard, is easily understandable.

Having said this, I must add immediately that problems in dynamic macroeconomics, so long as they are intended to be economics, cannot avoid also dealing with the world of values, and that our task is a peculiarly difficult one of combining the two aspects in an appropriate manner.

Marx's solution, as is well known, was to set up a two-department *tableau* for the economy as a whole. The principle of con-

1. JOHN MAYNARD KEYNES, *The General Theory of Employment, Interest and Money*, London: Macmillan, 1936, pp. 38-39.
2. See ROY F. HARROD, *Towards a Dynamic Economics*, London: Macmillan, 1948, pp. 28-34.

solidation which he adopted was twofold. On the one hand, he divides all the products into producers' goods and consumers' goods. This is a division from the standpoint of *material use* of the product and actually transcends specific modes of production. That is to say, such a division exists under socialism as well as under capitalism. On the other hand, Marx divides all the products into three components of *value*, namely, constant capital (C), variable capital (V), and surplus value (S). This represents a division which is characteristic of capitalism. Constant capital subsumes the cost of raw materials, fuel, and depreciation, and is so called because these items are considered to go into the value of the product without changing their value-magnitude. Variable capital refers to capital reserved for payment of wages, and is so called because it is the category which is considered to be the source of all the new value created and thus finds its *raison d'être* only if it is variable. Surplus value is the part which, according to Marx, is a residue out of the new value created over and above the necessary payment for wages, that is to say, the part which is 'exploited by capitalists'.

When we apply these two principles of division to the total products of society, we obtain the following six aggregates, in which the subscript 1 refers to the producer goods sector and the subscript 2 to the consumer goods sector:

$$C_1 + V_1 + S_1$$
$$C_2 + V_2 + S_2$$

Here in its simplest form is a *tableau* of commodity circulation. It is a *tableau* because these six categories are mutually interrelated in such a way that each of them constitutes at once (i) an aliquot part of the particular kind of product in the real aspect, i.e., either producer goods or consumer goods, (ii) a specific item in the value aspect, i.e., either constant capital, variable capital, or surplus value, and finally (iii) a demand for the particular kind of product in the real aspect, i.e., again either producer goods or consumer goods. In this way, the *tableau* becomes self-contained, where each item in the value aspect is in itself a demand for the product specific in the *tableau*.

The significance of this circularity becomes obvious if we

visualize the case of a non-capitalist world. Under socialism, for example, it is conceivable that the cost of labor-power becomes insulated from the demand for consumer goods by workers. The amount of purchasing power given to specific workers may be governed by principles which are not directly inherent in the cost structure. It is, in fact, one of the most important characteristics of capitalism that what is a cost item constitutes a direct demand for something. Thus the reduction of wage rates, while perhaps improving the cost-price maladjustment, results *ipso facto* in the shrinkage of effective demand. Marx's *tableau*, though quite simple, brings out this mechanism quite explicitly.

We can, of course, advance a step toward realism and introduce the fact of saving or accumulation into the Marxian *tableau*; but its fundamental character undergoes no change. Then, surplus value (S) divides itself into the part reserved for capitalists' consumption (Sk), the part destined to demand for producer goods (Sc), and the part destined to demand for additional labor power (Sv). And now the *tableau* may be rewritten as follows:

$$C_1 + V_1 + Sk_1 + Sc_1 + Sv_1$$
$$C_2 + V_2 + Sk_2 + Sc_2 + Sv_2$$

The manner in which these categories are related to each other can best be brought out by stating the condition of smooth exchange which would enable the system to go on without either overproduction or underconsumption. In order that the supply and demand for each kind of product be equal, it will be sufficient if the equation

$$V_1 + Sk_1 + Sv_1 = C_2 + Sc_2$$

is satisfied.[1]

It is true that we can draw on the implications of this equation to make a number of significant statements related to the nature of accumulation, for example, as regards the dependence of the proportion into which the total labor force is divided into

---

1. One can easily satisfy oneself that this is the case by equating the supply side with the demand side for each sector and cancelling the identical terms from both sides.

two sectors upon such factors as (1) the rate of surplus value (S/V), (2) the organic composition of capital (C/V), and (3) the rate of accumulation (Sc/S). But we shall not go into details here.[1]

One more point I should like to make is in connection with the needed distinction between the real and value aspects; that is, in critique of the lately fashionable use of aggregate production functions of the Cobb-Douglas type in estimating the degree of contribution by technical progress toward raising the productivity of labor.[2] The basic model assumes that technical progress, as well as capital and labor, contribute toward expanding total products (i.e., the real aspect); but it also assumes that the resulting product is exhaustively distributed between the two factors of production: capital and labor (i.e., the value aspect). With such a model, buttressed by a few simplifying assumptions, it has been 'discovered' that 'more than half the increased output recorded in historical statistics seems to be a "residual" attributable to scientific advance rather than to thrift and capital formation'.[3]

The basic confusion here is that an attempt is made to allocate relative contributions by several essential elements (in the real aspect) to production from the pattern of distribution (in the value aspect) characteristic of the capitalistic mode of production in the classical form.

In particular, the difficulty lies in the choice of units for capital in the aggregate Cobb-Douglas function. Aware of this difficulty, Johansen proposed a model which, according to him, did not require statistical figures for the stocks of capital in the empirical analysis.[4] Still, he had to resort to 'the cost associated with the use of capital', which is none other than the rate of profit, i.e., a ratio which, no matter how unambiguous it may be, still presupposes

1. This problem will be taken up in detail in Chapter Two.

2. I discussed this problem in greater detail in an article, SHIGETO TSURU, 'The Effects of Technology on Productivity', in *Problems in Economic Development*, edited by EDWARD A. G. ROBINSON, London: Macmillan, 1965.

3. PAUL A. SAMUELSON, *Economics*, p. 703.

4. LEIF JOHANSEN, 'A Method of Separating the Effects of Capital Accumulation and Shifts in Production Function Upon Growth in Labour Productivity', *The Economic Journal*, December 1961, pp. 775-782.

a particular way of measuring the denominator, capital. Between the restrictive concept of capital as a factor consistent with the aggregate Cobb-Douglas function and the concept of capital conventionally used in the calculation of the rate of profit, there is a long series of bridges that have to be crossed; and few of them are easy to cross. Let us postulate, for example, a world in which there is only one kind of machine. As noted by Solow, 'ideally what one would like to measure is the annual flow of capital services'. Now, a machine, like a laborer, has a finite life of its own. So long as it is in active use, it can be assumed to render more or less the same 'quantity' of service every year. But the *value* of a machine, which is relevant to the profit rate calculation, depreciates as it nears the end of its life. One might try to get around this difficulty by taking the gross stock instead of the net stock. But then, a change in the durability of the machine could affect the gross stock magnitude without changing the 'quantity' of current services rendered.[1] Secondly, the performance capacity of a machine, like a laborer, can be improved through technological progress without any change in durability or in the number of labor-hours required in production. Should such a machine not be counted in the Cobb-Douglas function as a multiple of the simple machine? Thirdly, compare two machines identical in every respect (including their durability and age) except that one is drawn from an economy with a higher product-wage rate. As Joan Robinson pointed out, 'the value of the two machines is different, and the investment required to create them is different. A difference in value remains if we deflate them by the wage rate, for in two economies with different product-wage rates the rate of profit and therefore, the rate of interest, are different'.[2] Furthermore, the real world makes use of a thousand and one different types of machines, both substitutive and complementary. A formidable number of problem arises here. In addition, the

1. On this point Solow says that 'there is nothing to be done about this': ROBERT M. SOLOW, 'Technical Change and the Aggregate Production Function', *The Review of Economics and Statigtics*, August 1957, p. 314.
2. JOAN ROBINSON, 'The Production Function and the Theory of Capital – A Reply', *The Review of Economic Studies*, n. 62, 1955-1956, p. 247.

concept of capital that is relevant to the profit calculation sub-sumes not only fixed capital but also working capital. Some economists would, even now as in the classical era, prefer to include what Marx called 'variable capital' (wage payment in advance of the sale of products) as a part of capital.

In other words, capital is essentially a value concept; and one cannot escape from its value implication as affected by the rate of interest, the time pattern of wage rate changes, etc., unless we assume a radically simplified economy of one-type machine with no technological change.

On the other hand, the real or physical aspect of production can only be described and does not easily render itself to abstract analysis. Whatever the type of economic system a society may have, the process of production in the society as a whole involves the exertion of effort by all kinds of men, with differing qualifications, who operate upon nature with objects fashioned out of nature in the circumstance of natural endowment and social environment not necessarily uniform everywhere. Operating workers, at any point in time, may be endowed with heritage, both technical and cultural, which is the accumulation passed on from their forefathers. Those selected few who are in the position of making decisions for a producing unit may have an aggressive outlook conditioned by the social milieu or by their innate propensity, and again they may not have it. Language is no less a factor in the situation, as can easily be surmised from the comparison of the following three countries: Japan, with the phoneticized media; China, with innumerable characters requiring years to master; and India, with a multi-lingual heritage not adapted yet to modern science and technology. It should be mentioned, moreover, that the problem of material balance in terms of use-values is quite relevant to the real or physical aspect of production.

Once we turn to the value aspect of production we cannot escape, in our discussion, from the framework of a particular economic system in which production is carried on. In general terms we could say that the value aspect of production would have the following components, all expressed in the same unit so that the addition is feasible:

$$\text{(Cost of raw materials and fuel)} + \text{(Replacement cost)}$$
$$+ \text{(Value added)}.$$

But how this unit comes about is dependent on the mode of production (as, for example, competitive pricing in a private enterprise economy or accounting pricing in a centrally planned economy) and how the value-added component is distributed among various categories is certainly not independent of the class relations of the society. In a feudal society, for example, the ruling class could claim a sizable portion of the value added on the basis of their *status* without in any way participating in the production process. In a capitalist society, at least in theory, knowledge as such does not receive its own marginal product, although few will doubt the substantial contribution it makes in the real or physical aspect of production. In a centrally planned economy it is perfectly possible to deliberately calculate the *value* reward for 'knowledge' in approximate accord with its obvious contribution in the real aspect. Again, the rentier income, as Keynes observed, may well be a historically transient category even within the framework of capitalism. Capitalism may well be a most efficient economic system; but to admit this does not absolve us from recognizing the efficacy of specific value relations which characterize different modes of production.

Technological progress, too, has its real and value aspects. Whether it takes place in the Soviet Union or in the United States, its real aspect can be described in almost exactly the same way. How to describe it, probably, would be the task of an engineer who would have to focus upon multiple causal relations in which the development of basic science, quality of labor, specific resource endowment, etc., would all have to be brought in. Essentially, the nature of this task is a description which ends up with a demonstration that the ratio between the physical output and the labor (both direct and indirect) input has risen – the ratio which we usually call 'the productivity of labor'. In such discussion of the real aspect it is not necessary that the unit of labor shall be in terms of the abstract concept of historically unchanging simple labor. In fact, it is generally understood that here labor is in terms of the biological unit which commonly changes its quality over time. Focusing our attention on this ratio, we can pose an inquiry as to relative contributions of various *real* factors to the rise of the ratio. A number of factors which are relevant may be enumerated:

A. education and training which enhance the quality of labor;

B. public health and medical services in general which contribute toward maintaining the continual effective performance of operating workers;

C. cultural amenities whose function is to raise the morale of workers;

D. industrial harmony which can elicit a greater degree of cooperation from the working class than the lack of it;

E. the improvement in the media of communications, including the modernization of language;

F. social and political tensions of constructive character, including what Rostow called 'reactive nationalism';

G. social innovations in the sense of 'new methods of inducing human beings to compete and cooperate in the social progress' (Kuznets);

H. technological innovations of both 'proper' and 'derived' types.[1]

I. the mere increase in the scale of production entirely apart from any technological change.

It is hard to deny that each one of these factors, in varying degrees in different historical circumstances, has been relevant in raising the productivity of labor; and it is probably harder to assign them quantitative weights in a given situation.

In the Japan of the last quarter of the nineteenth century, when the country is said to have accomplished the Rostovian 'take off' with remarkable speed, factors like (A), (E), and (F) above were undoubtedly of major importance, making it possible to achieve the 4 to 5 percent annual growth rate with a net investment ratio of less than 10 percent. A value relation like the capital-output ratio is bound to reflect such specific circumstances

1. Cf. CHARLES KENNEDY, 'Technical Progress and Investment', *The Economic Journal*, June 1961, p. 294.

of the country in the real aspect. And as long as we confine our attention to the real aspect, it is not very meaningful to ask what percentage in the rise of labor productivity was due to technological innovations and what was due to the increase in the 'quantity of capital' per worker.

The history of economic doctrines is replete with examples of theoretical attempts to draw out implications of institutionally conditioned socio-economic categories in terms of *a-social* (physical and/or psychological) factors. Such attempts lose sight of the specific laws of motion of an institutional system like capitalism and tend to induce one to close one's eyes to the evolutionary character of the system. The valuable lesson we can still draw from Marx is his emphasis on the efficacy of institutional factors upon what we call 'economic phenomena'. Thus Marx may be said to be an institutionalist *par exellence*.

CHAPTER TWO
The Methodology of Aggregates: Keynes vs. Marx

The methodology, characteristic of Karl Marx, of distinguishing between the real aspect and the value aspect, and at the same time integrating the two aspects, is best illustrated in his reproduction scheme about which I briefly referred to in the previous chapter. The significance of this methodology as exemplifying the institutional commitment of Marx can probably be grasped better by contrasting Keynes' and Marx's treatment of economic aggregates.

Modern society, in its economic aspect, presents itself as an interrelation of a tremendously large number of economic units. One kind of theoretical consolidation of these units or another has been practised since the birth of economics as a scientific discipline. Doctrinal survey would reveal how, since Quesnay's time, such consolidation of economic units has undergone a historical evolution.

Products of consolidation usually pertain to society as a whole and are called, in recent economic literature, simply 'aggregates'. The set of aggregates most widely used in modern economic discussion is, of course, the one associated with the economics of John Maynard Keynes. Let us refer to them as 'Keynesian aggregates'.

It is often said that the problem of aggregates is purely definitional and that one set of aggregates, if defined in terms of objective facts, can always be translated into another set. Though this latter proposition is frequently valid,[1] it is hardly true that the problem of aggregates is purely definitional. Consolidation is a way of organizing manifold data; it is the anatomy of the economic organism. It is natural that a specific consolidation, by resulting in a correspondingly specific fixation of our subject matter, may direct attention toward certain problems and away from others, and that it may even exercise an influence on the

---

1. SHIGETO TSURU, 'On Reprodution Schemes', Appendix to PAUL M. SWEEZY, *The Theory of Capitalist Development*, New York: Oxford University Press, 1942.

arrived at solution. To give an example, it is sufficient here to recall the terminological climate of the Böhm-Bawerkian capital theory, owing to which it was long denied that the elasticity of demand for labor could have a value smaller than one. To ascertain precisely at which point an error creeps in is not, alas for our science, a logical problem *simpliciter*. More than two alternative representations of a certain subject matter cannot only be compatible but are often complementary, as are projections of a multi-dimensional object from different angles. Conflict, however, becomes especially patent when we enter the realm of practice, for there it is necessary to test empirically the relative effectiveness of alternative approaches. What may appear theoretically to be only two sides of a shield finds its counterpart in practice as two opposing policies. A recent, though relatively minor, example of this kind is the controversy between the cost-adjustment and the effective demand schools of business cycle control. Often, of course, the conflict in practice goes deeper than this, for the fundamental reorganization of society may become involved.

As for the essentials of the Marxian aggregates, I have already made a summary statement in the previous chapter; but it may be repeated here to say that the Marxian *tableau* for the case of extended reproduction consists of two departments: producer goods and consumer goods, thus:

$$C_1 + V_1 + Sk_1 + Sc_1 + Sv_1$$
$$C_2 + V_2 + Sk_2 + Sc_2 + Sv_2$$

and that in order for the supply and demand for each kind of product be equal, it is sufficient that the equation

$$V_1 + Sk_1 + Sk_2 = C_2 + Sc_2$$

be satisfied.

Now superficially, this system of Marxian aggregates could easily be translated into Keynesian terms. Although in many ways the Keynesian aggregates are much more complex than the Marxian, in one respect they are simpler. That is, in the Keynesian system the degree of consolidation is still more thorough than in the Marxian case. Thus, to establish a bridge between the two systems, we first need to add the categories of the two sectors of Marx and obtain (note: $C_1 + C_2 = C$, and so on):

$$C + V + Sk + Sc + Sv$$

which is the total output, A, of Keynes.[1] His A_1, or enterpreneurial transactions, can be written as the sum of C and Sc. On the other hand, his G', or the net value conservable from what was on hand at the begining of the period (if we may ignore his B' as insignificant), is equal to the sum of C and V, while the means of production on hand at the end of the period, his G, consists of C, Sc, V, and Sv. Labor-power bought is included among the means of production, inasmuch as it is an asset in the sense of a renderable service and may be regarded as the limiting case of 'goods in process'.

Equivalent expressions for such terms as user cost, U, investment, I, income, Y, saving, S, and consumption, K, can easily be derived from the above. In the definitions of Keynes:

$$U = A_1 + G' - G \text{ (ignoring B')}$$
$$I = G - G'$$
$$Y = A - U$$
$$S = A_1 - U$$
$$K = A - A_1$$

Translated into Marxian categories:

$$U = C - Sv$$
$$I = Sc + Sv$$
$$Y = V + S + Sv$$
$$S = Sc + Sv$$
$$K = V + Sk + Sv$$

Take for example the equality: $Y = V + S + Sv$ (in which $S = Sk + Sc + Sv$). It appears that, first, the Keynesian Y, or national income, subsumes not only the wages bill (V) and surplus value (S), both which exhaust the 'value added' in the period, but also *additional* expenditure on labor-power (Sv) paid

---

1. JOHN MAYNARD KEYNES, *The General Theory of Employment, Interest and Money*, chap. 6.

out of the surplus value, and, secondly, that 'consumption' and 'saving-investment' overlap to the extent of such expenditures. In other words, Sv is registered twice as income and appears to be only once exchanged against goods. There is no mystery, however, once we make explicit the position of the commodity, labor-power, in the network of circulation. In the strict logic of capitalism, additional labor-power is just as much a part of the net national product as would be, for example, a new robot-machine. Two metamorphoses of Sv, therefore, have two distinct counterparts in the form of a commodity, once in labor-power and secondly in consumer goods.

The Keynesian consolidation is explicit as regards the so-called 'service industries' of which labor-power is a constituent, but does not admit labor-power, which is a 'producer good', into the category of investment goods. This difficulty is overcome, however, by imparting labor-power with a character of 'goods in process'. The moment new labor-power is purchased, it presumably commences to take part in the process of production; and to the income, disbursed against the labor-power, corresponds the limiting case of 'goods in process' as a part of investment.

This kind of comparability, even if perfect, is of course not very significant. In the paragraphs to follow I shall try to indicate some of the more important differences in methodology which should not be lost sight of in using the aggregates of either school. But here we may stretch our comparison a step further and try to see additional possibilities by way of finding formal similarities between the Marxian system and that of modern economics.

For this purpose, let us reproduce the equation

$$V_1 + Sk_1 + Sv_1 = C_2 + Sc_2$$

which, as it may be remembered, was the condition for the smooth reproduction of an economy which accumulates. Now if we define:[1]

s = the rate of surplus value, or the ratio of S_1/V_1 which is assumed to be equal to S_2/V_2;

1. SHIGETO TSURU, 'Marx's Tableau Economique and "Underconsumption" Theory', *Indian Economic Review*, February 1953.

$r_2 =$ the organic composition of capital, or the ratio of C_2/V_2;

$h =$ the proportion between the value of variable capital in the second sector and that in the first, or the ratio of V_2 over V_1. (If the wage rate is the same in both sectors, it indicates the proportions in to which the total labor force is divided between the two sectors.);

x_1 (or x_2) = the ratio of Sc_1 (Sc_2) over S_1 (S_2), we may rewrite this equation as:

$$sx_1 + shx_2 - (1 + s - hr_2) = 0$$

solving this equation for h, we obtain:

$$h = \frac{1 + s - sx_1}{sx_2 + r_2}.$$

This equation tells us that when there is balanced growth in the economy, the proportions into which the total labor force is divided between the two sectors, producer goods and consumer goods, namely h, is governed in a specific manner by three factors: (1) the rate of surplus value, s; (2) the 'propensity to save' or 'the propensity to invest' in the two sectors, x_2, and x_2; and (3) the organic composition of capital in the consumer goods sector, r_2. From this equation we can say definitely that, when the rate of surplus value rises, the proportion of the labor force going into the consumer goods sector must become smaller than before; when the 'propensity to invest' rises, assuming that $x_1 = x_2$, the said proportion also must decline; and, when the organic composition of capital in the second sector rises, the result is the same.

Now it will not be too far-fetched to compare these three factors with the famed three dynamic determinants of Harrod.[1] Our first factor here, the rate of surplus value, or s, is roughly a ratio of profit income to wage income; hence, its rise corresponds exactly to what Harrod calls 'the shift to profit', his second dynamic determinant. Our second factor, the 'propensity to invest', or x's, is quite similar, with only inconsequential differences, to his first determinant, the propensity to save, although the

---

1. Cf. Roy F. Harrod, *The Trade Cycle: An Essay*, Oxford: Clarendon Press, 1936, pp. 88-101.

latter is formulated explicitly as a relation between two contiguous periods. Our third factor, the organic composition of capital in the second sector, or r_2, focuses our attention upon the relation which Harrod chooses to call 'the amount of capital used in production', his third dynamic determinant. In terms of these concepts, one may recall that Harrod stated the following:

(i) Suppose that representative income-receivers save the same proportion of their increment of income as they previously saved of the income of the day before. (ii) Suppose that there is no shift to profit. (iii) Suppose that the productive methods for which the new capital goods were designed are the same as those previously employed. On these conditions consumption on the present day will rise in the same amount as that which the new capital goods were designed to provide, and this experience seems to justify the present rate of advance.[1]

Harrod is not speaking in terms of the proportion in which the total labor force is divided into the two sectors. But in both cases, that of Marx and of Harrod, the question implicitly asked is the same; namely, what are the factors which determine the proportion in which the national product is divided between consumer goods and producer goods as the economy advances steadily. Since the two men dealt with basically the same problem, it is not at all accidental that the correspondence between them appears to be almost perfect. What Harrod is saying in the above quotation is, in fact, what Marx would say, in our terminology, that h does not change if s, x's and r_2 remain constant. Harrod, of course, goes further and speculates for those cases where s, x's and r_2 change. For example, 'if people saved a large proportion of their increment of income or there were a shift to profit on the same day, . . . so far as these two determinants were concerned, consumption would advance less than the capital goods increased on the given day'.[2] In our terminology, this means that when s and x's rise h has to decline. Harrod's reasoning concerning the case of a rise in 'the amount of capital used in production' is slightly more complicated, but the con-

1. *Ibid.*, p. 90.
2. *Ibid.*, p. 91.

clusion comes to the same thing as the one obtained above in connection with the Marxian schema.

Thus the correspondence between the two systems is quite uncanny. But we cannot stop here. We must not fail to note the point of basic contrast between the two as regards the methodological position which the three determinants (s, x's and r_2) occupy. In Marx's model, they are variables or parameters implicit in the structure of his aggregates, and hence are formulated with explicit reference to the specificity of capitalism. Harrod, on the other hand, by setting these factors apart as forces independent of the system upon which they impinge, is obliged to fall back upon *a-social* generalizations for the explanation of the characteristic behavior of the determinants. Thus, the propensity to save is a 'fundamental psychological law'. The shift to profit and its positive sign are regarded as due to the joint operation of the laws of diminishing returns and of the diminishing elasticity of demand. And finally, the amount of capital used in production, barring short-run fluctuations, is made dependent upon inventions.

Through the apparent similarities on a certain restricted plane between Marx and Harrod, we immediately see a number of differences which are fairly basic. One of them is the difference in efficacy attributed to what may be called 'parametric adjustments' in the system.

A typical capitalistic process can be visualized as a cluster of 'parametric adjustments'. Each economic unit, be it a household or a firm, is independent of each other and, being such an infinitesimal part of the whole, is typically confronted with prices, wages, the rate of interest, etc., over which each economic unit singly has no control. In other words, these quantities (prices, wages, etc.) present themselves to economic units as parameters. For its part, the economic unit has no way of perceiving directly the state of economic conditions relevant to its action *except through* its contact with those parameters. Thus, it watches changes in them and adjusts itself to them presumably according to one kind of maximization principle or another. When, for example, there is an epidemic of cow disease, consumers do not and need not know about it. The number of cattle slaughtered inevitably will decline and the price of beef will rise. Consumers, finding the price of beef relatively dearer, will make a 'parametric adjustment' and shift their demand to chicken or pork. So long as competition is perfect, 'parameters' will fully and instantaneously reflect changes in data and call forth necessary adjustments on the part of economic units. It is in this manner that economic units, each independently enjoying the prerogative of freedom (and in spite of the fact that they are separated from relevant economic data by a cloud of 'parameters'), are considered to comprise a society in which maximum economic welfare can be maintained even while the objective conditions continue to change. Therefore, modern economic theory made much of the mechanism of 'parametric adjustments' and has built extremely intricate doctrines around the concepts of elasticities (indicating the manner of response of economic units to parametric changes) and flexibilities (indicating the manner of response of parameters to changes in data).

In the Thirties, however, the long-standing confidence in the positive function of 'parameters' gradually waned. For one thing, such phenomena as rigidities of wages, inflexibility of monopoly prices, and artificial control of exchange rates, coming to our attention all at once, have shaken our confidence in the presumed harmony in the system.[1] At the same time, certain statistical studies drew the attention of economists anew to the regularities of income effects which seemed to stand out much more clearly than the patterns of 'parametric adjustments'. In the words of Paul Samuelson:

Among the most striking uniformities yet uncovered in economic data are the relationships between various categories of expenditure and family income . . . In fact, so strong are these income effects

1. There is also a more general point which was expressed by NICHOLAS KALDOR as follows: 'It is now fairly generally recognized . . . that the price mechanism, even under the most favourable conditions, can register only some of the gains and losses which result from any particular piece of economic activity; there is a cluster of effects (what the economists call the external economies and diseconomies) which escape the net of price-cost measurement'. Appendix to WILLIAM H. BEVERIDGE, *Full Employment in a Free Society*, London: Allen and Unwin Ltd., 1944, p. 401.

that it is very difficult to find empirically the influence of price, the variable customarily related to demand by the economic theorist.[1]

In other words, the time was ripe for the emergence and rapid acceptance of the type of aggregative analysis propounded by Keynes in his *General Theory*. And, for a while, there arose a sharp division among the ranks of economists between those who would emphasize the income effect and slight the problem of cost-price adjustment and those who would give far greater weight to the efficacy of cost-price relationships. Even then, however, the most ardent of Keynesians would not ignore entirely the relevance of 'parametric adjustments' to many of the analytical problems. As time passed, the sharp contrast initially drawn gave way gradually to an attempt at synthesis and then to a tendency to place the crude aggregative analysis in its proper place.

The Marxian approach, on the other hand, is radically different in this regard. Marx himself was keenly aware of the important place which such categories as prices, the rate of interest, etc., occupied in the working of a capitalist system. Thus he repeatedly brings out the point that commodities, for example, appear to be an independent entity which naturally seem to possess the attribute of price to which men passively react. He does not deny the effectiveness of price categories, nor the process of 'parametric adjustments' which could be analyzed in an objective manner. But he is more concerned with the social relations among men which are hidden behind what appear to be natural attributes of things. Marx, of course, regarded the capitalist system as only one stage in the development of human societies, and he was especially eager to pin down the historically specific characteristics of capitalism as distinguished from other modes of production. Thus for him it was much less important to analyze the forces which determined the magnitude of value than to seek the reason why the product of human labor took the specific form of commodities under a capitalistic system.

---

1. PAUL A. SAMUELSON, 'A Statistical Analysis of the Consumption Function', Appendix to chap. XI of ALVIN H. HANSEN, *Fiscal Policy and Business Cycles*, New York: Norton and Co., 1941, p. 250.

And his answer to this question was: 'Only such products can become commodities with regard to each other as result from different kinds of labour, each kind being carried on independently and for the account of private individuals'.[1] In this type of society, the specific manner in which men are socially related to each other cannot be directly grasped, but instead, expresses itself through various quantitative relations among commodities, money, etc., and imparts upon the latter the appearance of being an independent social agent. Marx characterized this deceptive aspect of the commodity society as the 'fetish character of commodities'. In his own words: 'The character of having value, when once impressed upon products, obtains fixity only by reason of their acting and reacting upon each other as quantities of value. These quantities vary continually, independently of the will, foresight and action of the producers. To them, their own social action takes the form of the action of objects, which rule the producers instead of being ruled by them'.[2]

Marx felt it quite natural that what he called 'bourgeois economists', being unable to pierce through this fetishism, were mainly concerned with the quantitative analysis of 'the action of objects' which appeared to rule the producers, for they took it more or less for granted that capitalism was an immutable social relation and did not find it necessary to question the specific characteristic of the system as such. Since this was his major concern, Marx deliberately slighted the quantitative analysis of value and of its fluctuations, but developed his theory largely on the assumption of what Marshall would call 'long-run normal

---

1. KARL MARX: *Capital*, vol. I, Chicago: Charles H. Kerr and Co. [c. 1909]-1921, 1918, p. 49. In a similar vein he also wrote: 'As a general rule, articles of utility become commodities only because they are products of private individuals or groups of individuals who carry on their work independently of each other' (*ibid.*, pp. 83-84). Paul Sweezy elaborated on this as follows: 'The exchange relation as such, apart from any consideration of the quantities involved, is an expression of the fact that individual producers, each working in isolation, are in fact working for each other ... What finds expression in the form of exchange value is therefore the fact that the commodities involved are the products of human labour in a society based on division of labour in which producers work privately and independently'. PAUL M. SWEEZY, *The Theory of Capitalistic Development*, New York: Oxford University Press, 1942, p. 27.

2. *Ibid.*, p. 86.

price'. Thus his discussion of *tableau économique*, which appears toward the end of the second volume of *Capital*, is conducted throughout on the assumption that commodities are exchanged strictly at their value or at the 'long-run normal price'. In other words, 'parametric adjustments' have no place in the stage of abstraction where Marx took up his aggregative analysis.

It is quite important to emphasize this point because there have been so many attempts to make mechanistic use of Marx's *tableau* to provide a set of premeditated conclusions. The most visionary of these attempts is that of Henryk Grossmann, who tried to prove, on the basis of Marx's scheme of extended reproduction, the inevitability of breakdown of the capitalistic system.[1] What he did was to produce a general equation, on a set of rigid assumptions as to the rate of increase in the wage-bill and constant capital (approximately, user cost), giving us the number of years which would elapse before capitalists' income would no longer be sufficient to cover the required amount of net investment. Using the same notation we have given earlier and designating by n the number of years before the 'breakdown' comes, we may rewrite Grossmann's equation as follows:[2]

$$
n = \frac{\log\left(\dfrac{S - \dfrac{Sv}{V}}{r_0 \cdot \dfrac{Sc}{C}}\right)}{\log\left(\dfrac{100 + \dfrac{Sc}{C}}{100 + \dfrac{vS}{V}}\right)}
$$

1. See HENRYK GROSSMANN, *Das Akkumulations- und Zusammen-bruchsgesetz des kapitalistischen System*, Leipzig: C. L. Hirshfeld, 1929. Actually, of course, his theorizing was a specific product of the contemporary controversy and perhaps should not be criticized out of that context. He was originally trying to challenge Otto Bauer by carrying out to the logical conclusion the set of assumptions which Bauer employed in criticizing Rosa Luxemburg. As such, Grossmann's critique of Bauer contained an element of truth. In fact, however, Grossmann raised to the point of absurdity the common mechanistic error of a whole train of economists starting with Tugan-Baranowsky who made Marx's *tableau* serve a purpose for which it was never intended.

2. r_0 stands for the organic composition of capital for the economy as a whole in the initial period.

Thus if we assume, with Otto Bauer, that the rate of surplus value is unity throughout, that the organic composition of capital in the initial period is two, that constant capital increases at the annual rate of 10 percent $\left(\text{i.e., } Sc/C = \dfrac{10}{100}\right)$, and that the wage-bill increases at the rate of 5 percent $\left(\text{i.e., } Sv/V = \dfrac{10}{100}\right)$, then $n = 33.5$; that is to say, after approximately thirty-four years, capitalists' income would become insufficient to meet the required rate of accumulation.

This reasoning illustrates most strikingly the case of complete abstraction of 'parametric adjustments'. It is the essence of the price mechanism to register various tensions and disequilibria within the system, thus calling forth appropriate 'parametric adjustments' on the part of economic units (firms and households). Convulsive movement of the economy, which we call business cycles, is nothing more than an expression of such an adjustment process; and Marx would have considered absurd the extension of his logic of abstract *tableau économique* to a theory of breakdown without first going through many steps of concretization which certainly would have included the matter of 'parametric adjustments'. In other words, it must be strictly borne in mind that Marx's scheme of reproduction, or the framework within which his aggregative analysis is conducted, is highly abstract and does not permit indiscriminate attempts at manipulation.

The caricature which Grossmann made out of Marx's reproduction scheme is the culmination of a series of controversies conducted in terms of an all too mechanistic use of the categories in Marx's *tableau*. If one ignores parametric adjustments of any sort and assumes, as Rosa Luxemburg does, that the propensity to save is always 50 percent in both the producer goods and the consumer goods sectors, it becomes easy enough to show, by giving appropriate arithmetic examples, that effective demand will become insufficient to absorb all the final goods produced. Rosa Luxemburg's insight in recognizing this problem of effective demand is certainly not itself sterile, as Mrs. Robinson has pointed out.[1]

1. JOAN ROBINSON, 'Introduction', in ROSA LUXEMBURG's *The Accumulation of Capital*, London: Routledge and Kegan Paul Ltd., 1951.

But the use which Luxemburg made of the Marxian *tableau* in 'proving' the point is quite arbitrary and actually oversteps the limits which Marx himself carefully imposed upon the *tableau*. Thus it was not difficult for Otto Bauer to 'prove' the possibility of smooth reproduction on the very assumptions which Luxemburg employed, namely (1) that the propensity to invest is the same in both sectors, and (2) that the organic composition of capital rises as time goes on (or the capital-output ratio rises as time goes on).[1] So long as we confine ourselves within the logic of Marx's *tableau*, smooth reproduction is possible, as we have seen earlier, if the equation

$$sx_1 + shx_2 - (1 + s - hr_2) = 0$$

is satisfied. Luxemburg's problem boils down to the question of whether this equation can be satisfied when $x_1 = x_2$ and s and r_2 rise with time. It is easy enough to show that there is nothing in the logic of Marx's *tableau* to indicate that the steady growth will be upset by these assumptions.

In other words, it would not be correct to make too much use of the *tableau* in the form Marx left us. If we wish to address ourselves to a kind of problem with which modern economics concerns itself, Marx's reproduction scheme in itself does not give us an answer. The Marxian system must be further extended by incorporating a theory of 'parametric adjustments' in a manner consistent with the basic framework of the Marxian theory.[2]

One of the significant differences in the methodological character of aggregates between Marx and Keynes lies in the direction in which *abstraction* is carried out. Marx's intention was to represent, as simply as possible, the specific interrelation of aggregates which is characteristic of capitalism, whereas Keynesian aggregates do not necessarily concern themselves with the specif-

1. Otto Bauer, 'Die Akkumulation des Kapitals', *Die Neue Zeit*, vol. 31, n. 1, 1913.
2. An interesting attempt was once made by Professor Kei Shibata in this direction: see a series of articles in English he published in *Kyoto University Economic Review* in the first half of 1930s, or, in a more complete form, in his two-volume work: *Theoretical Economic* (in Japanese) *Riron Keizaigatu*, Tokyo: Kobunsha, 1935, 1936; see also my criticism of a part of his theory in 'Marx's theory of the Falling Tendency of the Rate of Profit', *The Economic Review*, July 1951.

icity of capitalism. They are designed primarily to assist in accounting for the level of total employment under the simple assumption that it is proportional to the net national product. A similar purpose, with differing assumptions, once gave rise to such concepts as 'wage-fund' and 'subsistence-fund' (Böhm-Bawerk). These concepts made us focus upon that aggregative quantity which controlled the demand for labor in a capitalist society. Keynes has reoriented our attention to the other side of the shield, so to speak, namely, to the simplest functional relation between the demand for various types of goods and the level of total economic activity – a relation which appears to transcend the specificity of capitalism.

Thus his first task was to carry through certain abstractional operations which would cut through complex appearances and to distil such aggregative quantities as might be independent of the capitalistic accounting method. The result is the Keynesian concept of national income which has only one dimension, that of being *consumable sooner or later*. The part which is consumed during a given period is called 'consumption', while the remainder, in whatever physical form it may be, is called 'investment'. Conceptually, this set of aggregates is perfectly unambiguous. To any type of society, be it primitive-tribal or socialistic, we may apply them and refer to the ratios between them by means of such terms as 'the propensity to consume', 'the propensity to invest', etc. The Keynesian aggregates gain this simple unambiguity by sacrificing certain distinctions which other systems of aggregates may be capable of making. In particular, they are indifferent to what Marx would call 'the metamorphosis in the realm of commodity circulation'. For example, x amount of consumer goods can either be assumed to have been sold or unsold and national income is in no way affected. This is because $Y = A - U$. And y amount of producer goods can be assumed to have been either sold or unsold and investment is in no way affected. For $I = G - G'$. Again, z amount of exports could just as well have been left unsold and remained in the warehouse of disappointed sellers, and national income would have remained the same.

In fact, the contrast between Marx and Keynes can be brought out most sharply in connection with the definition of investment. The definition of investment from the Keynesian standpoint is given by Samuelson as follows: 'The importance of investment consists in the fact that it involves disbursal of income to the factors of production while not at the same time bringing to the market goods which must be currently sold'.[1] Thus, from this point of view, the accumulation of inventories has the same function as the construction of new plant and equipment because such accumulation no less than the latter 'involves disbursal of income to the factors of production while not at the same time bringing to the market goods which must be currently sold'. Export surplus also has a similar function, as does the government deficit. In other words, Keynesian investment is defined mainly from the standpoint of its multiplier aspect and subsumes all kinds of economic acts which may be quite dissimilar to each other with respect to their productivity aspect. As such, it is no doubt a very convenient concept for short-run analysis, especially since it is a highly operational concept and lends itself to relatively easy statistical measurement. But once we try to apply it to a slightly longer-run analysis of dynamic character, its shortcomings become immediately apparent. The failure to take note of this limitation has led Mr. Hicks, for example, to construct a highly unrealistic theory of trade cycle with the concept of 'autonomous investment' which, like pyramid-building, absorbs savings without adding to productive capacity. Nowadays, of course, such unrealism is no longer tolerated by many; and we have a number of doctrines of economic dynamics, even in the camp of what may be regarded as the Keynesian school, which give a prominent place to the productivity aspect of investment activities. Domar's σ effect is one such example.[2] But when we try to incorporate the productivity effect of investment into our theory, we immediately realize that we must re-examine the concept of investment itself and make it theoretically a much more abstract concept than when we use it in the multiplier

1. PAUL A. SAMUELSON, 'The Theory of Pump-Pricing Re-Examined', *American Economic Review*, September 1940.
2. EVESY D. DOMAR, 'Expansion and Employment', *American Economic Review*, March 1947, p. 46.

analysis. Pyramid-building, for example, must be deducted from it. When we do this, we come closer to the concept of accumulation in the Marxian *tableau* which is throughout expressed in terms of value and is placed in the schema in such a way as to produce the *dual* effect of both creating effective demand and adding to productive capacity. The original concept of investment in the Keynesian aggregates is indifferent to the differing effects on productivity or to short-run occurrences of character other than those affecting effective demand.

Apparent indifference to distinctions of this kind does not mean, however, that the Keynesian system is altogether blind to them. Here lurks an important difference between Keynes' method of abstraction and that of Marx; and it is worth our brief examination. As Marx proceeds with his model, the indifference to certain distinctions on a given level of abstraction means the absence of these distinctions in the model itself at that level. For Keynes, *the very strength of his abstraction lies in the fact that the reality in its entire complexity is contained in it though only in a one-demensional projection.* Concretization of the system for Marx is typically the process of successive approximation. For Keynes, it is to change the angle of projection. Thus, whatever distinctions the Keynesian aggregates *appear* to be indifferent to, they are in fact contained in them implicitly and make themselves explicit on another plane of projection. For example, instead of distinguishing in *aggregate* between investment financed out of dishoarding and investment financed out of current saving, Keynes would call both of them simply investment when projected on the plane of aggregates but would take care of the distinction on another plane as between diminutions in liquidity preference and increases in the marginal efficiency schedule of investment.

In short, in point of contrast, aggregates themselves are neutral in the Keynesian system to the specificity of capitalism, viz., reduced to the simplest common denominator, as it were, for all types of society. The special relationships among aggregates which are characteristic of capitalism are squeezed implicitly into the form of function; the consumption function, the liquidity function, the marginal efficiency schedule of investment, etc. By the use of such terms as 'propensity' and 'preference' the impression is created, if only unwittingly, that these relations among aggregates are analogous to personal reactions on the conscious level and therefore are direct, and that they too were independent of the particular system of economy which they are used to analyze.

However, to say, for example, that the consumption function is a relation between aggregates analogous to personal reactions on the conscious level is not exactly correct. It is realized that, *theoretically speaking*, aggregate relations in modern economics are essentially *derived* relations, that is to say, deduced from household or firm relations.[1] But this fact creates a fresh theoretical problem. In the case of economic problems related to microeconomic units, the principle of maximization (whether of utility or of profit) helps us derive a meaningful theorem, thus enabling us 'to determine the nature of the changes in our unknown variables resulting from a designated change in one or more parameters'.[2] A large part of the body of economic doctrines today is dependent on the use of some kind of extremum position in arriving at a *theoretical* conclusion. The aggregate relation such as the consumption function, on the other hand, had initially been established as an empirical relation based upon statistical observations and has no claim for theoretical stability except inasmuch as it is continually supported by facts. The failure of economic model-building in 1945 illustrates this methodological character of aggregate relations. Thus, although Keynesians make much use of macroeconomics, they must fall back upon microeconomics for giving *ultimate theoretical* foundation to macroeconomic theorems. It is for this reason that Duesenberry states that 'aggregate relations which can be deduced from household or firm relations I shall call *fundamental* aggregate relations'.[3] Thus, the theoretical basis of Keynesian aggregates reduces itself finally to those relations between scarce means

1. See James S. Duesenberry, *Income, Saving and the Theory of Consumer Behavior*, first published as Harvard Economic Study, n. 87, Cambridge, Mass.: Harvard University Press, 1949; reprinted as a Galaxy Book, New York. Oxford University Press, 1967, 1949, p. 72.

2. Paul A. Samuelson, *Foundation of Economic Analysis*, 1st edition, Cambridge, Mass.: Harvard University Press, 1947, p. 7.

3. James S. Duesenberry, *Income, Saving and the Theory of Consumer Behavior*, p. 72, italics added.

and alternative uses which form the foundation of modern theoretical economics and which actually transcend any specific characteristic of the capitalist mode of production.

The Marxian aggregates, on the other hand, are not as operational as the Keynesian ones. The former appear mid way in Marx's theoretical journey from the most abstract discussion of value to the more concrete elucidation of crises and other typically capitalistic phenomena. Thus, such concepts as the rate of surplus value and the organic composition of capital which can be expressed directly as relations between aggregates are not necessarily susceptible of statistical treatment. In the form presented in Marx's *tableau*, aggregate relations cannot be subjected to empirical testing. They are theoretically pure concept. For example, the reproduction scheme as discussed in the second volume of *Capital* is constructed on the basis of the following assumptions: (i) that all the products are exchanged at value (i.e., long-run normal price); (ii) that there are only two classes of people, capitalists and workers; (iii) that workers consume all of their income; (iv) that there are sufficiently large numbers of capitalists in one field to permit perfect competition to take place; (v) that it is a closed economy; (vi) that there are only two kinds of commodities, the producers' good and the consumers' good, and the turnover period of capital is the same in both sectors; (vii) that there is no change in technical coefficients; (viii) that capital does not move between the two sectors, that is to say, the saving of the capitalists in the first sector is invested only in the first sector, and similarly for the second; (ix) that there is no durable capital equipment whose useful life extends beyond one period; (x) that there are no inventories; (xi) that money functions only as a means of circulation; and (xii) that wages are paid in advance of the sale of the products to whose production the workers contribute. In other words, the Marxian aggregates depict the bone structure, as it were, of the capitalistic circular flows as seen through X-ray, whereas the Keynesian aggregates show us the delineation of our subject matter as projected on a one dimensional plane.

The fact, however, that the Marxian aggregates are theoretical does not imply that it is possible to manipulate the elements

34

of the *tableau* to prove any particular theorem which is not already implicit in the structure of the *tableau* itself. In this sense, the Marxian aggregates by themselves do not claim to possess much deductive value. They are rather to serve for illustrative purposes, pointing out to us the nature of interdependence among various categories in the social circulation of a capitalist economy. And it is quite significant that, in serving this purpose, the *tableau* is divided into two sectors: producer goods and consumer goods. This is not the same thing as the distinction between investment and consumption. This latter distinction is a division of *net* national product, whereas the former is a division of the *gross* product of the society. In fact, the difference between Marx and Keynes in this respect is much more significant than is commonly supposed.

The Keynesians have made the concept of national income (or net national product) the pivot of their aggregative analysis and worked out a set of nice theoretical relations, such as the multiplier, acceleration, etc., with the aid of this concept. And the rationale of using the net concept in economic analysis seems to be further reinforced by the fact that it corresponds also to the index of welfare magnitude. National income has long been a measure of economic welfare, and, as such, even Marxians would not object very much. But the question is whether it is equally efficacious as *a tool in the economic analysis* of a capitalist society. To formulate our problem in terms of net concepts is as if to study the functioning of a certain organic body in terms of flows of energy which go in and come out of that body. Since this approach does not probe into the workings of the internal structure of the body, it is not possible to 'tag' a particular output as coming out of a particular input. What we do is watch, at the point of spigot, so to speak, what flows in and out of the body, and relate these flows to each other. Thus any relation between aggregates, such as consumption to income, has to be regarded only in terms of 'a flow during a period coincident with the flow of income during the same period'.[1] The method has undoubted

---

1. ABBA P. LERNER, 'Saving Equals Investment', *Quarterly Journal of Economics*, February 1938.

merits. It enables us to formulate macroeconomic relations in the simplest possible manner and at the same time gives us a strategic category in the form of money flow. At the same time, it makes us close our eyes to the functioning of the internal structure itself, which, far from being solely technical, possesses specifically economic characteristics under capitalism. It has the capacity, for example, of 'making mills to make more mills' for a time. It can distend itself or shrink without necessarily registering corresponding changes in net flows. The Marxian *tableau*, on the other hand, focuses our attention, again in the simplest possible manner, on the logic of this internal structure under capitalism by incorporating the value relation of C plus V plus S into the *tableau*. This method corresponds to the basic understanding of Marx that under capitalism production is not for the purpose of ultimate consumption but for the continuous maximization of profit. The contrast in this respect is more material than it initially appears. Although Keynesians do say that 'expenditure creates income and thus employment', they will not say that 'expenditure' provides the *motivating force* of production and further production. Marx would say, however, that the competition of capital striving toward the maximization of profit provides in itself a motive force for accumulation and technical progress; and such an orientation, which dispenses with either the acceleration principle or a special theory of investment function, is directly reflected in the construction of the Marxian *tableau*.

It was pointed out earlier that the *tableau* form of aggregates enables us to follow through the so-called dual aspect of investment, i.e., the aspect of creating effective demand and that of increasing productive capacity. It is possible for Keynesians to say that 'if investment today, however large, is equal to that of yesterday, national income of today will be just equal and not any larger than that of yesterday'.[1] Such a statement naturally follows from the Keynesian equation of income determination:

---

1. EVESEY D. DOMAR, *'Espansion and Employment'*, p. 40.

$$Y = C\,(Y) + \bar{I}$$
$$\Delta Y = \Delta C + \Delta I$$
$$\Delta Y = \left[\frac{\mathrm{I}}{\mathrm{I} - \dfrac{\Delta C}{\Delta Y}} \right] \Delta I$$

It is obvious from this last formulation that without an increase in investment there will be no increase in national income. Suppose from year to year, several years in succession, net investment remains the same – net investment referring, for example, to an addition to plant and equipment with the implication that productive capacity is increasing. Even in this case, the above equation suggests that there will be no growth in national income.

On the other hand, it is impossible for Marxians to visualize a case of 'extended reproduction' in equilibrium, i.e., the case of an economy which accumulates at all, without a corresponding increase in net national product. Investment in the Marxian *tableau* is traced in its dual aspect to its proper destination in a manner consistent with certain significant constraints which are specified within the *tableau*. Furthermore, since the *tableau* makes explicit the relation between C and Sc (or roughly, between 'user cost' and the net addition to capital), our attention can easily be directed to the position which replacement (or depreciation) occupies in the mechanism of social circulation. It is only recently that this problem has become considered an integral part of the mechanism of a growing economy.

At times, I may have drawn too sharp a distinction between the treatment of aggregates by Marx and that by Keynes. Most of these points of difference were in fact sharp at the time when Keynes first brought out his theory of effective demand. Since then, many refinements and improvements have been added to the original scheme of simple Keynesian aggregates. Some of them have been actually in the direction of narrowing the difference between Marx and Keynes on this matter. Dissatisfaction with the analysis conducted solely in *net* concepts is a most notable example. I suspect that in the future the reproduction scheme of Marx will draw the attention of a larger number of academic

37

economists than in the Thirties. But there is one last fundamental difference in methodology which still divides the modern and Marxian schools of economics. The point may be illustrated from Mr. Harrod's methodological dicta in his book, *Trade Cycle*. So far as we can gather from his scattered remarks in that book, his methodology may be paraphrased as follows: we go as far as we can by means of an *a priori* method, the principal tool of which is introspection; and if *a priori* yields no more, we revert to observed facts and see what actually does happen. When, however, he reverts to observation, it is in order to look for an answer to a specific question which introspection alone is incapable of solving. It is characteristic of him to say, for example:

> The shift to profit has been shown ... to depend on two factors. ... It would be rash to say much *a priori* about the operation of either of these laws (the law of diminishing returns and the law of diminishing elasticity of demand) ... But experience is that there usually is a shift to profit in a pronounced upward movement.[1]

And this is enough for him to assert that there is a shift to profit. But, as Schumpeter would say, 'this is a problem to be solved, not a datum to be accepted.[2] The problem of social science only begins, to say the least, at the point where introspection leaves off.

What is conspicuous in Harrod is his extreme reluctance to recognize the existence of objective laws of *social* relations. It is more than a playful dictum, we may venture to guess, when he says: 'We are reluctant to suppose that man's course of endeavour can be governed by something so superficial and artificial as his own banking system.[3] If, however, society, as a subject matter of scientific endeavor, is a complex of qualitatively distinctive relations on its own level and not simply an amalgam of individuals who compose it or of atomic matter to which all existence may be reduced, it will be wisdom in methodology to presume that social relations are governed by objective laws which are not reducible to psychological and physical laws and

---

1. Roy F. Harrod, *The Trade Cycle*, p. 92.
2. Joseph A. Schumpeter, *Business Cycles*, New York: McGraw-Hill, 1939, p. 188.
3. Roy F. Harrod, *The Trade Cycle*, p. 4.

which are beyond the reach of introspection, however discerning it may be. A theoretical edifice in social science built upon such a presumption is evidently under a handicap in developing its 'analytical apparatus' if by the latter is meant an apparatus to account for the phenomena of a particular society in terms of the specific laws pertaining to that society. Marx's major concern was precisely the elucidation of the specific laws pertaining to a capitalist society, and his aggregates are tools of analysis for that purpose designed primarily to lay bare the social circulation of capital.

CHAPTER THREE
Marx vs. Schumpeter on Business Cycles

Let me quote a paragraph which sounds very much like the one written by an institutional economist:

> The capitalist process not only destroys its own institutional framework but it also creates the conditions for another . . . The outcome of the process is not simply a void that could be filled by whatever might happen to turn up; things and souls are transformed in such a way as to become increasingly amenable to the socialist form of life. With every peg from under the capitalist structure vanishes an impossibility of the socialist plan.

This is from the pen of none other than J. A. Schumpeter[1] who, as a self-confessed admirer of 'elegance' in theoretical constructs, is seldom identified in the camp of institutional economists. Furthermore, his inclination toward historical analysis is more clearly stated in the opening chapter of his posthumous work as follows:

> What distinguishes the 'scientific' economist from all the other people who think, talk, and write about economic topics is a command of techniques that we class under three heads: history, statistics, and 'theory'. The three together make up what we shall call economic analysis.
>
> Of these fundamental fields, economic history – which issues into and includes present-day facts – is by far the most important. I wish to state right now that if, starting my work in economics afresh, I were told that I could study only one of these three but could have my choice, it would be economic history that I should choose. And this on three grounds. First, the subject matter of economics is essentially a unique process in historic time. Nobody can hope to understand the economic phenomena of any, including the present, epoch who has not an adequate command of historical *facts* and an adequate amount of historical *sense* or of what may be described as *historical experience*. Second, the historical report cannot be purely economic but must inevitably reflect also 'institutional' facts that are not purely

1. JOSEPH A. SCHUMPETER, *Capitalism, Socialism, and Democracy*, 2nd edition, New York: Harper and Brothers, 1947, p. 162.

economic: therefore it affords the best method for understanding how economic and non-economic facts *are* related to one another and how the various social sciences *should* be related to one another. Third, it is, I believe, the fact that most of the fundamental errors currently committed in economic analysis are due to lack of historical experience more often than to any other shortcoming of the economist's equipment.[1]

As can be seen from these quotations, there was an unmistakable inclination on the part of Schumpeter to respect institutional or historical analysis. True, Schumpeter was in many ways a paradoxical character. It is well known that he, along with Irving Fisher and Ragnar Frish, was responsible for establishing the Econometric Society in 1930 and that one of his earliest published articles was 'Über die mathematische Methode der theoretischen Ökonomie' in which he wrote:

> I must say that so far I have not heard any objections which appeared sound to me, none which – would have shaken my belief that on this method rests the future of economic theory as science – as Jevons put it 'if Economics is to be a science at all, it must be a mathematical one'.[2]

To his last day, Schumpeter harbored an ambition to work out a neat mathematical formulation of his theoretical architecture. And yet, on the other hand, more than any other modern economist engaged in the research of business cycles, he had a clear awareness of the inseparable connection of business cycles and the capitalist process, carrying it to a most systematic and elaborate form. The subtitle to his work, *Business Cycles*,[3] placed in apposition, reads: 'A theoretical, historical, and statistical analysis of the capitalist process'; and the very first sentence which ushers us into the volume is again his major theme in succinct formulation, to wit: 'Analyzing business cycles means neither more nor less than analyzing the economic process of the capitalist era'. This

1. JOSEPH A. SCHUMPETER, *A History of Economic Analysis*, edited from manuscript by ELIZABETH BOODY SCHUMPETER, New York: Oxford University Press, 1954, pp. 12-13, italics in the original.

2. JOSEPH A. SCHUMPETER, 'Über die mathematische Methode der Theoretischen Ökonomie', *Zeitschrift für Volkswirtschaft*, vol. 15, 1906, p. 37.

3. JOSEPH A. SCHUMPETER, *Business Cycles*, McGraw-Hill, 1939.

very remark is what Marx would have said. Therefore, it should be interesting to compare Schumpeter with Marx as regards the manner in which the phenomenon of business cycles is related to the institutional characteristics of capitalist society. This is the task I intend to pursure in this chapter.

Let us, then, first distil Schumpeter's imposing structure and try to grasp the crucial link by which capitalism and business cycles are inseparably connected in his theory.

There seems to be little question that the concept of *innovation* holds the key to the theoretical edifice of Schumpeter. He himself proposes as his 'analytic intention . . . to make the facts of innovation the basis of our model of the process of economic change'.[1] When thus informed, we are less concerned for our purpose with the precise content of the term innovation than with its relation to capitalism. We ask: Is innovation, as such, characteristic *only* of capitalism? Although he harps on the fact that innovation is what dominates the picture of capitalistic life, and although he stresses the point that it is a factor of change *internal* to the economic system, his answer is unequivocal: *innovation is no more confined to capitalist society than are changes in tastes*.[2] If, therefore, business cycles are uniquely associated with capitalism in Schumpeter's scheme of explanation, we must look elsewhere for the crucial connecting link.

This we seem to find in what he calls 'the monetary complement of innovation'; i.e., credit creation. On the one hand, we note that he qualifies his definition of capitalism[3] by stressing

---

1. *Ibid.*, pp. 86-87; Also cf.: 'Surely nothing can be more plain or even more trite common sense than the proposition that innovation, as conceived by us, is at the center of practically all the phenomena, difficulties, and problems of economic life in capitalist society and that they, as well as the extreme sensitiveness of capitalism to disturbance, would be absent if productive resources flowed . . . either in unvarying or continuously increasing quantities . . . every year through substantially the same channels toward substantially the same goals, or were prevented from doing so only by external influences' (*ibid.*, p. 87).

2. Cf. 'The entrepreneurial function is not confined to capitalist society' (*ibid.*, p. 223).

3. He defines that 'capitalism is that form of private property economy in which innovations are carried out by means of borrowed money, which in general, though not by logical necessity, implies credit creation' (*ibid.*, p. 223).

43

in particular the element of credit creation.[1] Neither the system of private property nor the element of entrepreneurship constitutes the distinguishing mark of capitalism. On the other hand, he is quite articulate in stating that credit creation renders an innovation which produces those changes in economic quantities associated with the prosperity phase; e.g., the rise in the prices of the factors of production, the rise of money incomes and of the rate of interest, and so on. Significantly enough, he goes on to show that these changes are absent if an innovation is carried out by means of savings or, under socialism, by an administrative order. This leaves no doubt as to the pivotal significance of *credit creation* in connecting business cycles with capitalism. *But is it the only link?*

It is doubtful that Schumpeter would give an unequivocal affirmative to this question. The stature of his analytical scheme implied in the subtitle of his book previously quoted leads us to suspect that the element of credit creation is too meager a creature to stand alone as the crucial connecting link. Perhaps we are not asking the right question. It may be that in Schumpeter's scheme of explanation capitalism and business cycles are related in such a way as not to permit the singling out of distinct connecting links. In order to pursue him, therefore, we should reorient ourselves in the light of his methodological dictum. The starting point of his explanation (of business cycle phenomena) is succinctly formulated by him as follows: If we observe that the event Y (business cycles) occurs in a set of 'real' phenomena X (capitalist society), 'it will not necessarily have meaning

---

1. Cf.: 'In the institutional pattern of capitalism there is machinery, *the presence of which forms an essential characteristic of it,* which makes it possible for people to function as entrepreneurs without having previously acquired the necessary means' (*ibid.*, p. 103, italics added).

Also cf.: 'We shall date capitalism as far back as the element of credit creation' (*ibid.*, p. 224).

What then is credit creation? It is the *ad hoc* creation of the means of payment for the purpose of enabling the entrepreneur to bid away from the use otherwise destined those factors of production which he requires for carrying out his innovation. 'The shifting of the factors is effected not by the withdrawal of funds . . . "cancelling the old order" . . . from the old firms, but by the reduction of the purchasing power of existing funds which are left with the old firms while newly created funds are put at the disposal of entrepreneurs' (*ibid.*, pp. 111-112).

to search X for a single cause of Y.[1] It is desirable rather to develop a conceptual schema X′, by which to handle X, and then ask the question whether or not X′ implies the occurrence of Y, and which of the properties of X′ are responsible for it. 'There is always meaning to . . . (such a) question.'[2] How then is his X′ developed?

His conceptual schema X′ is, in the first instance, embodied in the theory of equilibrium. This 'gives us, as it were, the bare bones of economic logic which, however abstract or remote from real life it may be, yet renders indispensable services in clearing the ground for rigorous analysis'.[3] Or it 'supplies us with the simplest code of rules according to which the system will respond'.[4] We are familiar with the concept of general equilibrium, to which Schumpeter proposes no fundamental amendment. In fact, as if to accommodate the traditional equilibrium analysis, he confines, as a matter of hypothesis, the 'innovating' activities to *new* men, *new* plants, and *new* firms and allows the traditional analysis to have maximum applicability in describing the responses to innovation by *old* firms which by definition do not resort to *creative* responses.

The theory of equilibrium, then, constitutes the basic mode of X′ and now he is able to speak of the '*necessity* of starting our analysis in perfect equilibrium'[5] and to maintain that the test of a theory (of business cycles) *as a fundamental explanation satisfactory in logic* is that it be able to show at least the possibility of a cyclical movement '*starting from a strictly stationary* process in which all the steadying forces and mechanisms of the system are perfectly intact'.[6] He rejects, therefore, the hypothesis that an economic system could, without any particular 'force' impinging upon it, work in a wavelike fashion merely by virtue

1. *Ibid.*, p. 34.
2. *Ibid.*, p. 34.
3. *Ibid.*, p. 68.
4. *Ibid.*, p. 68. Also cf.: 'Our understanding of the way in which the economic organism reacts to any given new event is unavoidably based upon our understanding of those equilibrium relations' (*ibid.*, p. 68).
5. *Ibid.*, p. 83, italics added.
6. *Ibid.*, p. 182, italics added.

of its structure.[1] It is clearly conceived by Schumpeter that an equilibrium mechanism as an apparatus of response does not by itself generate cycles, but the 'force' of innovation acts intermittently upon it and, by bringing into play the action of the equilibrium 'force', causes the characteristic features of the business cycle.

In search for crucial connecting links between business cycles and capitalism other than credit creation, we pose here our old question: Does the theory of equilibrium represent the *differentia specifica* of capitalism? If the apparatus of response as developed by the theory of equilibrium is germane to any type of economic system, be it capitalistic or socialistic, it cannot serve as a *crucial* connecting link between capitalism and business cycles, even if it is a necessary condition for the occurrence of the latter.

Schumpeter himself is consistent in refusing to use the term capitalism throughout his discussion of equilibrium. He speaks of 'economic system', 'economic logic', 'economic process', and 'economic organism', and strongly suggests the possibility of using the purest form of equilibrium analysis as a starting point of economic analysis for any type of society or even of individual household. To the extent he actually does this he is divesting his X' of the peculiar marks of X and forcing himself more and more to rely, for establishing the connection between X and Y, upon either the segregated factors of innovation and credit creation or the unformulated interstitial conditions of X. That he dates the phenomenon of business cycles as far back as credit creation, that he conceives of it in terms of multiple cycles, that for him there does not exist periodicity in the usual sense of the term – all these flow out of his segregation of particular factors which are theoretically made responsible for the occurrence of Y. It appears, then, that on his own admission his X' transcends the institutional limitations of X and, furthermore, is

---

1. See *ibid.*, p. 180, the first paragraph. Also cf.: 'The business cycles with which we are concerned ... are not analogous to the oscillation of an elastic string or membrane ... which, once set into motion, would, but for friction, go on indefinitely ... because they are due to the intermittent action of the "force" of innovation, by which the action of the equilibrium 'force' is each time brought into play' (*ibid.*, p. 175).

not directly responsible for the phenomenon of Y. Thus, in the final analysis, we seem to be left with only one crucial connecting link; i.e., credit creation.

Such logical distillation of Schumpeter's theory as presented above commits, of course, many oversimplifications in the process. Readers who take trouble in studying his volumes will find appeals made in numerous places to specific conditions of capitalism for the explanation of various aspects of the business cycle phenomena.[1] But his is not meant to be an eclectic theory which allows piecemeal explanation for individual aspects of the problem. We are led by his own methodological prescription to expect from him a simple and elegant skeleton-structure of a theory of business cycles. That he succeeds in constructing it through the formulation of a conceptual schema (X') may well be conceded. However, the crucial question, the answer to which remains in doubt, is *whether he successfully abstracts X' out of X such that it is at once differentia specifica of X and the explanatory tool of Y.* Doubt is cast, in other words, as to whether he succeeded in following his own methodological prescription. It may be questioned, however, if the theory of equilibrium is as neutral to institutional specifications as he seemingly implies. One may

---

1. For example, as regards the clustering of innovation, which aggravates the initial disturbance and *'enforces a distinct process of adaptation'* (*ibid.*, p. 101), we find him saying: 'If action in order to carry them [major innovations] out were equally open to all as soon as they became technically and commercially possible [which will be the case under socialism], those disequilibria would not be different from, and not more serious than, those which arise currently from changes in data and are currently absorbed without very great difficulties and without "revolutions" or upheavals' (*ibid.*, p. 97).

It may also be pointed out that the proposition that the igniting innovation strikes the system around the neighborhood of equilibrium and also the proposition that entrepreneurial activities slacken because of the impossibility of calculating costs and receipts in a satisfactory way are, aside from the question of their validity, founded on the implied horizon and economic rationality of bourgeoisie.

Also cf.: 'Our argument rests on (abstractions from) historical facts which may turn out to belong to an epoch that is rapidly passing . . . We assume not only private property and private initiative but a definite type of both; not only money, banks, and banking credit but also a certain attitude, moral code, business tradition, and "usage" of the banking community; above all, a spirit of the industrial *bourgeoisie* and a schema of motivation which within the world of giant concerns . . . and within modern attitudes of the public mind is rapidly losing both its scope and its meaning' (*ibid.*, pp. 144-145).

argue that the theory is nothing but an abstraction of the *capitalistic* apparatus of response *par excellence*, and that, being a refined abstraction of a one-sided phase, it possesses an appearance of generality and may actually permit a limited application beyond the confines of capitalism. One may follow this line of interpretation, and say that the methodical avoidance by Schumpeter of associating the equilibrium analysis with capitalism is dictated more by his theoretical zeal as such than by any positive endorsement on his part of the institutional neutrality of the equilibrium analysis. We may recall his apt simile that 'cycles are not, like tonsils, separable things that might be treated by themselves, but are, like the beat of the heart, of the essence of the organism that displays them'.[1] If by 'the organism' he means, as he must, a capitalist society, it is difficult, indeed, not to associate his basic theoretical apparatus of response with the specificity of that organism. If we are correct in thus reading between his lines, it must still be emphasized that Schumpeter fails to demonstrate with sufficient explicitness how his explanatory tools of Y flow necessarily from the *differentia specifica* of X.

When the fall of an apple was explained not simply in terms of its ripeness or the blowing wind but also in terms of gravitation, it marked an important step in the progress of physical science. The *terra firma* in the realm of social science is a prevailing and relatively intransmutable setup of society. Apparent permanence of any social setup often leads one to take for granted the specificity of the conditions which prevail under it. Science, which takes nothing for granted, is called upon to reveal, if true, the infirmity of the *terra firma* or, again if true, the transient specificity of capitalist society. The degree to which critical search in this respect is needed differs according to the types of problem we investigate. The recognition that the problem of business cycles is one of those problems which require the revelation of its connection to the specificity of capitalist society is the reputed strength of Schumpeter's theory. If his theory is found to leave still much to be desired, the explanation may be that his approach is *from business cycles to capitalism* and that, due to the complexity

1. *Ibid.*, Preface, p. v.

of the intermediate links, the consummate synthesis is too much to hope for. In contrast to his theory, we shall now examine that of Karl Marx, whose approach may be said to be the opposite of Schumpeter's, namely, *from capitalism to business cycles*.

Marx concerned himself principally with the basic analysis of the dynamics of capitalist society – a subject matter which is much wider in scope than the majority of modern economists would care to deal with. The fact that his theory of crises itself evolved on this wide base, as pertaining not to accidental abnormalities but to the normal course of economic development, is the reason for our special interest in Marx's contribution.

Although Marx placed a great deal of emphasis on the phenomenon of crisis, or the periodical breakdown, he was hardly less articulate in speaking of recurrent 'industrial cycles', by which, there seems to be no question, he meant what we have since become accustomed to calling 'the business cycle'. But if we figuratively represent the unfolding of a theory as consisting of a hierarchy of levels of abstraction ascending from the most abstract base of essentials to the height of manifoldly concrete phenomena, Marx would place the phenomenon of business cycles nearer to the top. Between this latter and the basic characteristics of capitalism he would intervene numerous steps of approximation only a few of which he attempted to elucidate. If at all, his contribution lay nearer as regards the base than as regards the top. In other words, the direction of his approach is *from capitalism to business cycles*. It is his methodological prescription that the general conditions of cyclical phenomena be demonstrated as developing out of the general conditions of the capitalist mode of production. How then does Marx formulate the defining characteristics of capitalist society?

Toward the end of the third volume of *Capital* we find him summarizing such characteristics into two foci:[1]

1. the prevailing and determining character of its products is that of being *commodities*;
2. the production of *surplus value* is the direct aim and determining incentive of production.

1. KARL MARX, *Capital*, vol. III, Kerr edition, pp. 1025-1027.

49

These we may take as our starting point and try to pursue their necessary implication in the direction of further concretization. By way of caution, it should be remarked that the two italicized expressions above must be registered in our minds in their specific Marxian context. Marx would maintain that, under all stages of society's development, human labor confronts itself with nature and man-made means of production to produce the means of consumption, but that the institutional form which this confrontation takes differs according to different stages of history, and that a *commodity* is a product of human labor taking one particular institutional form. Likewise with the concept of *surplus value*. Marx would say that, beyond a certain stage in the development of productivity, human labor is capable of producing surplus above the goods necessary for subsistence, but that the form which the surplus assumes and the way in which it is distributed differs according to different stages of history, and that *surplus value* is one particular institutional form of such a surplus occurring in one stage of society's development.

Of the two characteristics mentioned above, the first provides background for what Marx calls 'the possibility of crisis'. Commodity production pertains not solely to a capitalist society; but, by acquiring a *prevailing* and *determining* character, it forms a general background for the basic elements of capitalistic economic transactions. The implications of commodity production may best be elucidated in its contrast to the barter economy.

A barter economy can schematically be decomposed into a unit process of $P_1 - P_2$; that is to say, 'Product 1' is *directly* exchanged with 'Product 2'. The latter is the aim achieved by parting with 'Product 1'. Further, the connotation is reversible; for the person who parts with 'Product 2', 'Product 1' is the end result. The commodity economy, on the other hand, calling forth by its very nature the prevalent use of the general value form (money), splits this simple process of $P_1 - P_2$ into two, i.e., $C_1 - M$ and $M - C_2$ (where C denotes a commodity and M denotes money). M appears to be only an intermediary. But let us scrutinize what this implies. The producer of C_1 now produces it for the market where he expects to exchange it for money. He has no idea who wants it and how much of it is wanted. Communal decision or social consideration no longer shapes or supersedes his individual policy. The external world outside him presents itself only in the shape of a demand curve. Still his definite aim remains that of acquiring C_2. The movement which began with the entrance of C_1 into the market cannot come to rest until it ends in the acquisition of C_2 by the producer of C_1. But once he sells his C_1 for M, he is under no compulsion to buy C_2 immediately, nor from the person to whom he sold C_1. He can bring M home, wait for a few months, go to a neighboring town, and buy C_2 with M. In other words, M 'splits'[1] the process of $C_1 - C_2$ both *temporally* and *spatially*. And if the interval of time between the two complementary phases of the process, $C_1 - M - C_2$, becomes too great, if the cleavage between the sale and the purchase becomes too pronounced, the essential unity of the process asserts itself convulsively by producing a crisis. Thus arises the first possibility of crises.[2] Further elaborations on the first possibility are added as Marx makes more concrete his discussion of money; for example, the function of money as 'a means of payment', i.e., the function of acting as the measure of value and the realization of value at *two different* moments, strengthens and solidifies the possibility.

---

1. In using the transitive verb for M, we commit an oversimplification. C appears from the backstage of workshop onto the stage of the market, where plenipotentiary M directs it hither and thither. After it undergoes a metamorphosis into M, it makes an exit again into the backstage never to come back. But M constantly reappears on the stage, and seems to string a series of commodities into a chain *ad infinitum*. Thus the 'continuity of the movement is sustained by the money alone ... the result of the circulation of commodities assumes the *appearance* of having been effected, not by means of a change in the form of commodities, but thanks to the function of money as medium of circulation ... money seeming to set passive commodities in motion, transferring them from the hands in which they are not use-values into the hands in which they are use-values. Although, therefore, the movement of the money is merely an expression of the circulation of commodities, it seems as if, conversely, the circulation of commodities were only the outcome of the movement of the money' (*Capital*, vol. i, Paul ed., pp. 94-95). This point is especially important, because the fetish illusion of M being the culprit for all the evils of the exchange economy and the consequent advocacy of monetary measures as necessary and sufficient stems out of the failure to realize the importance of the context within which alone M can operate. The root, Marx would say, lies in the commodity economy itself.

2. Marx stresses the point that it is as yet only a possibility and warns against J. S. Mill's attempt to explain crisis by its possibility.

However, we shall not here pursue the chain of complications which follows this starting point; instead, we turn now to the second basic characteristic of capitalism and its relation to the phenomenon of crisis.

The second characteristic, the production of surplus value as the direct aim and determining incentive of production, can be telescoped into the unit movement of capitalist production schematized by Marx as:

$$M - C - C' - M' \quad (M' = M + \Delta M)$$

A capitalist starts with money capital, M, buys the means of production, C (including labor power), manufactures his product, C', and sells the same in exchange for M'. Unless M' is larger than M, the movement loses its basic *raison d'être*; in fact, the maximization of ΔM in relation to M is its direct aim. The movement starts with M and ends with M', quantitatively different but qualitatively identical. This permits the goal M' of the process (M – C – C' – M') to immediately become a new starting point, making it possible structurally to satisfy the self-perpetuating tendency for aggrandizement through the successive repetition of the process. Then there arises the possibility of treating such successive series of unit processes over time, each of which is conditioned by the specific time of turnover, as being composed of two unbroken series of M and M' which connect each point of time with a specific value of ΔM. The unity of the process C – M – C, achieved through having as an objective a consumer's good which by its very nature drops out of economic circulation, is now shattered. The apparent unity in the process of M – C – C' – M' is an abstraction, having no longer a restraining force as a unit process, because it is in the very nature of M, which is the goal of this process, to remain in circulation in order to fulfil its function of increasing its own value.

It is an essential aspect of capitalistic specificity, according to Marx, that the determining consideration which governs its (capitalism's) unit process is the uninterrupted expansion of ΔM, and *not* the satisfaction of social needs.[1] Therefore, the conditions

1. Cf.: 'The expansion or contraction of production ... is determined by profit and by the proportion of this profit to the employed capital ... instead of being

which promote or hinder the success of such an expansion constitute the subject matter of essential significance. This may be divided into two aspects which are 'separable logically as well as by time and space'[1] namely, (1) the conditions of the *production* of surplus value and (2) those of its *realization*. The first is concerned with the process of production itself while the second is the problem of sales.

With respect to (1), the conditions of the production of surplus value are primarily technological and permit the direct improvement at the hand of individual capitalists. The determining motive of capitalist production finds its expression in the constant effort on the part of individual capitalists to improve the technique of production. From the standpoint of society as a whole, the limitation to the production of surplus value lies in the number of the working population and the level of technological knowledge. But the objective consequence of this 'capitalistic' (in Böhm-Bawerkian sense) development, abstracting for the moment from the problem of effective demand, is the falling tendency of the rate of profit. This is visualized by Marx as an immanent *tendency* rooted in the capitalist mode of production itself. If the pursuit of profit maximization leads necessarily to greater and greater use of machinery, and if this in turn finds its expression inevitably in the falling tendency in the ratio of ΔM to the employed capital, a vicious circle is already evident. The falling tendency naturally evokes reactions to counteract it – reactions which are not necessarily free of a boomerang effect. But once the tendency becomes actuality, and the rate of profit does indeed fall, the motive power of the system receives a setback and the process of accumulation suffers. It is evident, if such is the case, that expansion can neither be smooth nor go on indefinitely.

With respect to (2), the conditions of the *production* of surplus value, however, are only one side of the shield. The conditions of its *realization* must now be examined. It is characteristic under

---

determined by the relation of production to social wants. The capitalist mode of production comes to a standstill at a point determined by the production and realization of profit, not by the satisfaction of social needs' (*Capital*, vol. III, Kerr edition, p. 303).

1. *Ibid.*, p. 286.

capitalism that claims on goods are derived not as a function of actual needs as in the economy of an individual family, but as a function of factor payments which are contracted or expanded in accordance with the ebb and flow of the profit-seeking activities of capitalists. It is a corollary of this capitalistic specificity that the aggregate size of such claims emerges as a result of atomistic decisions on the part of individual capitalists and thus cannot be controlled directly as an aggregate. In the eyes of individual capitalists, in whose hands lies the all-important decision as to the expansion or contraction of economic activities, the conditions governing the realization of their surplus value appear in the guise of a natural law standing outside their control.

Thus, the inherent tendency in capitalism to expand production and to improve productivity both in the interest of profit maximization, while incidentally exerting a relative downward pressure on cost-factor payments, is confronted with a basis of realization which is that it is not the business of a single capitalist to expand except incidentally to his action in pursuit of profit maximization. Therefore, this inherent tendency leads inevitably to frantic competition for markets among capitalists who expend huge sums in the form of selling costs and burst outside the bounds of a national economy, seeking forever the expanding market abroad.

Such reasoning forms the background for Marx's famed dictum:[1]

> The last cause of all real crises always remains the poverty and restricted consumption of the masses as compared to the tendency of capitalist production to develop the productive forces in such a way that only the absolute power of consumption of the entire society would be their limit.

In short, we have, on the one hand, the tendency, partaken by each capitalist independently, to enlarge the production of C' regardless of the fall in the value of the product and of the size of ΔM contained in C'; while, on the other hand, each capitalist seeks not only to preserve the value of the existing capital but also to expand it by realizing all the ΔM he produces.

1. *Ibid.*, p. 568.

Herein Marx finds the basic contradiction of the capitalist mode of production which tends constantly to upset the harmonious development of production. Capitalist production is continually engaged in the attempt to overcome this barrier of harmony, but it is inherent that it is overcome only by means which again place the same barrier in its way in a more formidable size. The solution, therefore, must be forcibly brought about by a breakdown which, through the destruction of values and the unemployment of resources, works toward the restoration of the objectively balanced relations. The *inevitability* of crisis is thus unfolded out of the second of the basic characteristics of capitalism.

Many links still remain before we even come to the point of concretion where Marx left off.[1] But we have traced far enough Marx's method of developing the concrete from the abstract, so that we may now appraise the contrasting aspects of the two theories under discussion.

It may be said, as was suggested earlier, that Schumpeter's approach was from business cycles to capitalism whereas Marx's was the reverse, from capitalism to business cycles; and it may be maintained on that ground that their theories are largely complementary and that whatever differences may exist between them must be discounted in view of the historically different intellectual milieus and the different apparatuses of analysis. However, the points of contrast thus far indicated are sufficiently far-reaching not to preclude the possibility of conflict between the two theories. As a preliminary to the formulation of a basic distinguishing feature between the two, we enumerate first a number of specific contrasting points on the commensurate plane which flow rather obviously out of our exposition above.

---

1. For instance, with the appearance of interest-bearing capital, the above movement sublimates itself into the simple process of $M - M'$. Then the movement of M as money capital develops its own autonomous laws and does not remain entirely passive to the movement of an individual capital each individually determined through the maximization principle and the given material conditions. Further on, the development of credit mechanism increases the degree of freedom with which component units of social reproduction can move about. It lends wings to them, partly aggravating and partly rectifying the disequilibrating tendency.

55

First, Schumpeter works on the hypothesis of an intermittent 'force' impinging on the otherwise stationary process, whereas Marx leaned more on the hypothesis picturing cycles as akin to self-perpetuating waves of adaptation.[1]

Secondly, related to the above is Schumpeter's tendency to regard the business cycle as a primary and logically pure phenomenon which manifests itself on the surface of complex reality only as *a tendency*. Marx, in contrast, regarded it as a projection, on a restricted plane, of varied complex phenomena, basically conditioned by, but so remotely separated from, the essential characteristics of capitalism that intermediate links of explanation were not amenable to nice theoretical formulation.

A third point of contrast may be cited as regards the dating of the historical beginning of the cycle. Schumpeter goes as far back as the occurrence of credit creation. Marx's criterion is much more structural. He writes:

This peculiar course of modern industry (a decennial cycle interrupted by smaller oscillations), which occurs in no earlier period of human history, was also impossible in the childhood of capitalist production . . . We began to witness that ever-recurring cycle only when mechanized industries thrust their roots deeply in the national economy and began to have overwhelming influence upon it, and through such development foreign trade acquired more prominence over internal commerce, leading to the extension of the world market over wide areas of America, Asia, and Australia, and also when the number of mutually competing industrial nations grew fairly large.[2]

1. Cf.: 'As the heavenly bodies, once thrown into a certain definite motion, always repeat this, so is it with social production as soon as it is once thrown into this movement of alternate expansion and contraction. Effects, in their turn, become causes, and the varying accidents of the whole process, which always reproduces its own conditions, take on the form of periodicity' (*Capital*, vol. I, Torr ed., p. 647). As Engels phrased it: 'Every element which works against a repetition of the old crises, carries the germ of a far more tremendous future crisis in itself' (*Capital*, vol. III, Kerr edition, p. 575, *fn*).

Also cf.: 'A crisis is always the starting point of a large amount of new investment. Therefore it also constitutes, from the point of view of society, more or less of a new material basis for the next cycle of turnover' (*Capital*, vol. II, Kerr edition, p. 211).

2. *Capital*, vol. I, Torr ed., p. 647. The second sentence in this quotation does not seem to appear except in the 1873 French (Marx editing) edition and the 1935 Russian edition of *Capital*, but is reproduced in *Das Kapital*, III, The Marx-Engels-

He considers these conditions to have been more or less satisfied around 1820.[1]

In the final analysis, however, these points of contrast, though significant in themselves, are corollaries of the difference which is more fundamental. This difference, in short, lies in the extent to which the distinctive implications of capitalist society are explicitly brought out and the manner in which they are made responsible for the phenomenon of business cycles. To elaborate on this point, it will be convenient to avail ourselves of the language used by Dr. Lange in comparing Marxian economics with modern economic theory.[2] He formulated the problem in terms of data and variables in economic theory, contending that Marx's success in long-run prognostications was due to his particular attention to the treatment of his data. Or, phrased otherwise, Marx regarded as variables of his system that which is generally considered as 'given' data by modern economists. To a degree, such a contrast holds true between Marx and Schumpeter. However, it is quite possible that two theories with differing horizons amount to the same thing when logical distillation is carried through. Conflict in theory exists if one contends a certain system of variables, A, B, and C, to be *sufficient* for the explanation of a certain phenomenon, while the other insists that another variable, D, is *necessary* for the explanation of the same phenomenon. Marx's explanation of business cycles *depended on the inclusion* of certain *institutional* factors into the category of variables – the inclusion of which is not essential for Schumpeter's explanation. Not to make explicit the specific institutional characteristics of capitalism was, for Marx, to give up the very task of explaining the phenomenon of business cycles. Schumpeter, on the other hand, carries out first the process of abstraction on

Lenin Institute edition, Nachtrage zum I. Band. 'America' is omitted from this last source, but is apparently to be found in the Russian edition according to VARGA's *World Economic Crises*, I, 1937 (in Russian), p. 4.

1. In speaking of the decade of the 1820s in his preface to the second edition of *Capital* (vol. 1), Marx wrote: 'Modern industry itself was only just emerging from the age of childhood, as is shown by the fact that with the crisis of 1825 it for the first time opens the periodic cycle of its modern life' (*Capital*, vol. 1, Torr ed., xxiii).

2. OSKAR LANGE, 'Marxian Economics and Modern Economic Theory', *Review of Economic Studies*, June 1935.

the capitalist process – the abstraction of which would, according to Marx, necessarily involve the throwing away of those elements which are responsible for crises – and then loads the responsibility for cyclical phenomena, not on the institutional characteristics, but on the act of innovation which in itself transcends the institutional specificity.

In conclusion, it must be stated that Schumpeter's edifice, though supported and embellished by countless references to concrete details of capitalist society, reduces itself logically to a theory which falls short of establishing a necessary connection between capitalism and business cycles, whereas the spadework which Marx carried out more than a century ago remains unchallenged and little improved. On the occasion of discussing the significance of Marxian economics for present-day economic theory, a modern economist said not so long ago:

In so far as the general methodological principle is concerned any effective extension of a theoretical system beyond its old frontier represents a real scientific progress.[1]

It is in this light that we have re-examined the two authors who are coincidentally joined in 1883 by one's death and another's birth.

---

1. WASSILY LEONTIEF, *American Economic Review*, March 1938, Supplement, p. 8.

CHAPTER FOUR
Institutional Economics in America: Veblen

It is generally agreed that American institutionalism was 'born', so to speak, with the impact given by Thorstein Veblen (1857-1929). Leon Ardzrooni, who edited Veblen's *Essays in Our Changing Order*, 1934, wrote in his Introduction:

> Veblen was in reality one of those rare men who may be said to have been ahead of his time – ahead in the sense that what he said and thought was destined to be accepted by succeeding generations though they were rejected by his own generation. 'Hence, he was lonely as an alien can be.'

Also, Wesley Mitchell (1874-1948) wrote shortly after Veblen's death, referring to the influence of that 'disturbing genius': 'no other such emancipator of the mind from the subtle tyranny of circumstance has been known in social science, and no other such enlarger of the realm of inquiry'.[1]

In spite of these laudatory words by his disciples, Veblen, along with American institutionalism, appears to have been either pushed into oblivion or regarded as unworthy in the current atmosphere of American academic circles. Paul Samuelson, for example, in the 12th edition of his standard textbook (*Economics*, 1985), omitted entirely a reference to institutionalism; and Robert Kuttner, in a recent contribution to *The Atlantic Monthly*, wrote:

> A generation ago economics was far more committed to observation, disputation, and its own intellectual history. The lions of the mid-century had lived through depression and war, had watched real economic institutions totter, had worked in economic agencies, and had appreciated the power of statecraft. Most of them are now gone. In the 1920s and 1930s an eclectic school of economics known as institutionalism flourished. Inspirad by Veblen, institutionalists were committed to the empirical study of corporations, banks, labor unions, and so on as concrete social organizations. Ironically, they were dis-

---

1. 'Research in the Social Sciences', in *The New Social Science*, University of Chicago Press, 1930, p. 5.

placed partly by econometricians, who promised a more rigorous empiricism. Institutionalists still exist . . . But few institutionalists are to be found at the fifteen or twenty elite graduate schools that turn out tenured faculty for one another. The very term has become a pejorative.[1]

It is probably pertinent to make a brief sketch of the historical background of the period when Veblen came onto the scene.

Veblen was born in Wisconsin in 1857 as a son of a poor Norwegian immigrant. The most active period of his intellectual career, that is, roughly from 1880 to 1905, coincided with a number of noteworthy events in American history. For one thing, the frontier, the significance of which Frederick Jackson Turner emphasized so much, practically came to an end by 1890; and in its place, attention was directed outward to overseas development as exemplified by the Spanish-American War at the turn of the century. At the same time, a new long-term wave of prosperity was ushered in from about 1897, i.e., what economists call 'the third Kondrachiev wave' characterized by innovations in automobiles and the chemical industry. On the one hand, concentration of capital, especially in the oil business under Rockefeller, went on unabated until the Sherman anti-trust law was enacted in 1890, though without much effect; and on the other hand a major trade union came into existence in 1881 in the form of the American Federation of Labor. The last quarter of the nineteenth century in America is often referred to as 'the Gilded Age' and was susceptible to social criticism of all kinds in which Veblen, along with Mark Twain, played a conspicuous role.

To begin with, Veblen did not start out as a student of economics. His education, which began at Charleton College and was continued at Johns Hopkins and Yale, was in the wide-ranging field of natural history, philosophy, sociology, and classical languages. It was not until after he married Ellen Rolfe in 1888 when he read, with her, Bellamy's *Looking Backward* that he shifted his professional interest into economic matters.

However, it is said that Veblen's impression of his father in his

1. ROBERT KUTTNER, 'The Poverty of Economics', *The Atlantic Monthly*, February 1985, p. 83.

childhood had made a strong imprint on his mind, which later crystallized itself in the form of a controlling dichotomy of 'industry' and 'business'. His father was a farmer with intense interest in agricultural techniques and instruments but was sadly unsophisticated in the matter of money-making and thus was a prey to scheming businessmen. Veblen respected his father's 'industry' and felt antagonistic to the world of 'business'.

'Industry' for Veblen is concerned with *making things* (i.e., work of engineers and technicians), while 'business' is concerned with *making money* through price differentials (i.e., work of traders and financiers). This dichotomy is central in Veblen's analysis of capitalistic society; and David Riesman aptly cited the movie 'The Big Carnival' as a Veblenian parable. In this tale,

> A man is pinned in a cave by falling timbers. For a cynical newspaperman, his plight is a 'find' and he proceeds to 'mine' the man out by drilling through the top of the mountain in which the cave is located, rather than going in through the direct, commonsense passage which would extricate him too soon and spoil his news monopoly – and spoil also the carnival-like monopolies of hawkers and other prehensile folk who are making a good thing out of the crowds who come to watch the drilling. In the course of these business-like proceedings, a matter-of-fact and experienced engineer-artisan appears, and asks why they don't go directly after the trapped man, who all this time is suffering and is further tormented by the pounding drills overhead. But the interloper lacks the gift of gab and control of communications channels (the 'state' is in on the deal, in the person of a blowsy sheriff who hopes for reelection from the publicity; so is a corrupt contractor who has close ties to the politician), and after making his point into the mike, the engineer is fended off by astute questioning – industry succumbs to business. But in the end business succumbs too; the trapped man dies, and as the Vested Interests have a falling out, the newspaperman loses his monopoly, and is shot by the dead man's rapacious wife.[1]

On the pages of many a writing, Veblen harped on this polarizing distinction between engineers and their allies on the one hand and absentee owners and others on the other. The former group

---

1. DAVID RIESMAN, *Thorstein Veblen: A Critical Interpretation*, New York: Scribner's Sons, 1953, p. 81.

is motivated by the 'instinct of workmanship' and 'idle curiosity', both considered as constructive elements in human life. The latter group, however, draws on predatory attitudes towards man; and while interfering with production on behalf of profits and inflationary credit transactions, members of the group vie with each other in spending their spoils in 'conspicuous consumption'.

This implies consumption designed exclusively to impress with the cost that was involved. Taste does not matter. And as Galbraith wrote, 'never after the publication of *The Theory of the Leisure Class* could a rich man spend with ostentation, abandon and enjoyment without someone rising to ridicule it as Conspicuous Consumption'.[1]

It should be noted that for Veblen, as for Marx, technology was the prime mover of socio-economic development, and further that its progress was cumulative and independent of the will or actions of the businessmen. But again similar, to Marx, Veblen thought that technical progress would bring in its wake institutional changes leading at first to a state of chronic depression, then to a monopolized economy in which profits are protected but human and material resources are persistently underutilized. Such a state of affairs in turn intensifies and sharpens a struggle already implied in the occupational division of society between industry and business.

Where the logic of this struggle would point to, Veblen was not quite certain at the time he wrote *The Theory of Business Enterprise* in 1904. In the final paragraph of that book he wrote:

Which of the two antagonistic factors may prove the stronger in the long run is something of a blind guess; but the calculable future seems to belong to the one or the other. It seems possible to say this much, that the full dominion of business enterprise is necessarily a transitory dominion. It stands to lose in the end whether the one or the other of the two divergent cultural tendencies wins, because it is incompatible with the ascendency of either.[2]

1. JOHN KENNETH GALBRAITH, *The Age of Uncertainty*, Boston: Houghton Mifflin, 1977, p. 61.
2. THORSTEIN VEBLEN, *The Theory of Business Enterprise*, New York: Menter Books, 1904, p. 400.

Essentially, this uncertainty remained in Veblen's mind until the end of his life. But the intervening period of imperialism, war, and chauvinism had apparently done its dreary work; and by the time he wrote 'Economic Theory in the Calculable Future' in 1925 he seems to have been more inclined to note the ascendency of the *business* side of the dichotomy, as can be seen from the following passage:

In the economic foreground stands, of course, the organization of business enterprise, the absentee owners and their agents, in whom vest by law and custom all initiative and discretion in economic affairs. And it is to this work of the business community that the economists are chiefly turning their attention. And such should presumably continue to be the drift and emphasis of economic inquiry and speculations in the calculable future, inasmuch as the promise of things as they run in the immediate present is, unmistakably, that the interests and exigencies of business traffic are and of right must be paramount. These things are visible, understandable, legitimate, and urgent; and like other men the economists are imbued with the preconceptions of the price-system, in terms of which these things are understandable and urgent; but in terms of which the other half, the technological half, of the current economic world is obscure and, at the best, subsidiary.[1]

Obviously, he was not approving 'business' against 'industry'; but, most likely, he was reconciled to the idea, toward the end of his life, that the profession of economists was bound to be 'drawn in for no other purpose and no other qualifications than such as are presumed to serve the bankers and traders of the nation as against outsiders'. This is because 'any technical advance can get a hearing and reach a practical outcome only if and in so far as it can be presented as a "business proposition"; that is to say, so far as it shows a convincing promise of differential gain to some given concern. So also the economist who ventures to take stock of anything in the technological way and to bring such facts into the framework of his theoretical structures will of necessity handle these matters as a "business proposition", as

1. THORSTEIN VEBLEN, *Essays in Our Changing Order*, ed. by LEON ARDZROONI, New York: The Viking Press, 1934, p. 11.

ways and means of differential gain for one business concern as against others'.[1]

Here is a thought offered on the dependence of technical advance upon the profit-oriented business enterprise – a departure from Veblen's erstwhile insistence on the dichotomy between 'industry' and 'business'. Throughout most of the writings of Veblen, the basic underlying view was that:

> The capitalist operated purely in the realm of finance, and his only relation to production is one of sabotage and obstruction; his object is to mulct the underlying population to the maximum possible degree and to waste the proceeds in ostentatious display. Meanwhile, despite the obstruction of capitalists, mechanical industry expands and becomes increasingly productive.[2]

Such a view led Veblen to regard the industrial engineer as the truly progressive factor in the modern economy and to postulate the existence of a basic conflict between the capitalist and the engineer. Sweezy pointed out four main weaknesses in this theory, namely:

(1) It ignores, or at least slurs over, the capitalist's fundamental urge to add to his wealth as distinct from consuming it; (2) it entirely fails to see that accumulation by the capitalist can take place only through the steady expansion of the means of production and employment of more labor; (3) consequently it fails to see that the capitalist in effect calls into existence the industrial engineer, pays him, and gives direction to his work, and finally: (4) it inverts the relationship of engineer to capitalist, which is in reality one of dependence of the former on the latter, and makes it appear as a relation of conflict.[3]

The first two points here are well taken and remained as weaknesses of Veblen's analysis of capitalism, but the latter two points mentioned by Sweezy do not seem to have lingered on toward the end of Veblen's life as we have seen in the quotation from his 1925 article on 'Economic Theory in the Calculable Future'.

1. *Ibid.*, pp. 13-14.
2. As summarized by PAUL M. SWEEZY, *The Present as History Essays and Reviews on Capitalism and Socialism*, New York: Monthly Review Press, 1953, p. 299. Originally written for *The New Republic* (25 February 1946) as a review of the 1946 of the reprint of Veblen's *On The Nature of Peace*.
3. *Ibid.*, p. 299.

In fact, there are signs in his later writing, such as *The Engineers and the Price System* (1921), that he became more realistic in appraising the relation between engineer and capitalist.

There seems to be little doubt that the appearance of Henry Ford contributed to this sense of realism on the part of Veblen. *The Engineer and the Price System* was written after Ford had gained national celebrity; and Veblen was obliged to make an admission in that book (p. 10) which somewhat compromises his life-long belief in the conflict between engineer and financier: he wrote that there exist

exceptional, sporadic, and spectacular episodes in business where business men have now and again successfully gone out of the safe and sane highway of conservative business enterprise that is hedged about by conscientious withdrawal of efficiency, and have endeavored to regulate the output by increasing the productive capacity of the industrial system at one point or another.

Ford was an engineer-businessman, and in a number of ways shared certain propensities with Veblen: such as (1) the hating of absentee ownership; (2) awareness of the enormous productive possibilities of American industry; (3) contempt towards smooth ways of modern business enterprise and modern social intercourse; (4) distrust on received realities ('History is bunk!'); (5) a romantic sympathy for the insubordinate underdog; and, finally, (6) a shy, sly, and evasive character. Veblen never mentioned Ford by name, but he must have regarded him as an enigmatic embodiment of his concept of ideal engineer.

Here, I may be permitted to indulge in a sort of digression and comment a little on Veblen's somewhat peculiar idiosyncrasy as an academic man.

Galbraith wrote: 'During his academic life he moved from Cornell to Chicago, to Stanford, to Missouri, to the New School in New York. All were glad to see him go; it is now the pride of all that he was there'.[1]

One of the reasons he was eased out of an institution was that he was inordinately attractive to women. He himself considered

---

1. JOHN KENNETH GALBRAITH, *The Age of Uncertainty*, p. 60.

it a problem. And once, when rebuked by President Jordan of Stanford for the offence he was giving to middle-class morality, he is said to have asked resignedly what a man could do when they (women) just move in with you.

There is of course a deeper reason for Veblen's incongruity with university administration. He thought that even a good and honest scholar, once in the president's seat, would soon become as corrupt a salesman of 'ponderous vendible intangibles' as any small-town banker, delegated by the board of trustees to give the institution an 'efficient, businesslike management'. In fact, Veblen recognized here the unfortunate role of the scholar-president, 'caught on the margin between God and Mammon, between science as a collective heritage and the business culture as a growing nastiness'.[1]

Veblen apparently felt that the universities could run themselves, once outside interference was removed, just as he thought that the economy could run itself, as a technical engineering problem, once vested interests were liquidated. Thus he listed university presidents as one of the superfluities of American society, along with prostitutes, advertising, hotelmen, the services of porters and retailers. We must say that he went a bit too far in this regard. He, maintaining a straight face, calculated that seven-ninths of the work done in a typical country town in the farm belt of America was dispensable as consisting of parasitic occupations. How he arrived at this figure of seven-ninths, no one seems to know.

However, here we are reminded of an extremely discerning passage we find in one of Karl Marx's writings:

A philosopher produces ideas, a poet poems, a clergyman sermons, a professor compendia, and so on. A criminal produces crimes. If we look a little closer at the connection between this latter branch of production and society as a whole, we shall rid ourselves of many prejudices. The criminal produces not only crimes, but also criminal law, and with this also the professor who gives lectures on criminal law, and in addition to this the inevitable compendium in which this same professor throws his lectures onto the general market as 'com-

1. David Riesman, *Thorstein Veblen: A Critical Interpretation*, cit., 104.

modities'. This brings with it augumentation of national wealth, quite apart from the personal enjoyment which . . . the manuscript of the compendium brings to the originator himself. The criminal moreover produces the whole of the police and of criminal justice, constable, judges, hangmen, juries, etc.; and all these different lines of business, which form equally many categories of the social division of labor, develop different capacities of the human spirit, create new needs and new ways of satisfying them. Torture alone has given rise to the most ingenious mechanical inventions, and employed many honorable craftsmen in the production of its instruments . . . The effects of the criminal on the development of productive power can be shown in detail. Would locks ever have reached their present degree of excellence had there been no thieves? Would the making of bank-notes have reached its present perfection had there been no forgers? . . . Crime, through its constantly new methods of attack on property, constantly calls into being new methods of defence, and so it is as productive as strikes for the invention of machines.[1]

In a more serious vein, however, Veblen did draw out an implication of wasteful expenditures in a capitalist society in the following manner:

The absorption of goods and services by extra-industrial expenditures which, seen from the standpoint of industry, are pure waste, would have to go on in increasing volume. If the wasteful expenditure slackens, the logical outcome should be a considerable perturbation of business and industry, followed by depression.[2]

In other words, he was aware of the role played by the 'institutionalization of waste' in maintaining business prosperity under capitalism.

Then, what prospects did Veblen hold for the future of capitalism? In answering this question, we will have to enlarge our purview of Veblen's thought to include his political theory. For him, as a matter of fact, the theory of capitalism was, almost from the outset, as much political as economic – a characteristic of an institutional economist, we may say. He had a theory of the state under capitalism, consisting of two basic aspects. First,

1. KARL MARX, *Theories of Surplus Value*, Moscow: Foreign Language Publishing House, vol. I, 1964, pp. 375-376.
2. THORSTEIN VEBLEN, *The Theory of Business Enterprise*, p. 120.

the state is the guarantor of the existing social order; and this means that its first and overriding duty is to safeguard property rights. Therefore, the state is in the hands of the propertied classes and will be freely used by them to protect and promote their own interests. Secondly, democracy of the western societies does not only not contradict this scheme of things but fits into it as an integral working part. 'A constitutional government is a business government . . . Representative government means, chiefly, representation of business interests'.[1]

On the face of it, such a theory of the state appears to closely resemble the definition which Marx and Engels gave to the bourgeois state in their *Communist Manifesto*. Veblen, however, differed from Marx and Engels in thinking that the state does not exclude the underlying population from the governing process for the reason that the business leadership would not be able to govern without 'the advice and consent of the common run'.[2] For this purpose, it would be necessary that the underlying population had been successfully conditioned to want the business leadership. Could this be guaranteed? Veblen did not answer this question directly except to point to, as stated earlier, the intensification and sharpening of a struggle already implied in the occupational division of society between industry and business. As to this 'struggle', there was an evolution in Veblen's thought from categorical concern with the occupational division between industry and business to an increasing reference to 'the effectual division – on class lines, between the absentee owners and the underlying population'.[3]

At any rate, Veblen was aware of a possible crisis which might come about in a capitalist society – a crisis which the business leadership could also foresee. Thus, he developed a theory regarding the counter instruments of policy to which the business leadership was expected to resort. Thus came his theory

1. THORSTEIN VEBLEN, *Absentee Ownership and Business Enterprise in Recent Times: The Case of America*, London: Allen and Unwin, 1923, p. 37.

2. THORSTEIN VEBLEN, *The Vested Interests and the State of the Industrial Arts*, New York: B. W. Huebsch, 1919, p. 16.

3. THORSTEIN VEBLEN, *Absentee Ownership and Business Enterprise in Recent Times: The Case of America*, p. 6.

of 'national integrity' (or plain nationalism) into the picture. It had two aspects, namely: (1) equating the interests of business leadership with those of the nation as a whole; and (2) adopting aggressive policies toward the outside world, accompanied by the militarization of society.

Related to the first of these points is the following remark by Veblen:

> By stress of this all-pervading patriotic bias and that fantastic bigotry which enables civilized men to believe in a national solidarity of material interests, it has now come to pass that the chief – virtually sole – concern of the constituted authorities in any democratic nation is a concern about the profitable business of the nation's substantial citizens.[1]

In this way, the government is enabled to secure popular support for a program devoted in the main to the furtherance of class interests.

On the other hand, however, and as mentioned earlier, the machine process, for Veblen, is the motor force of capitalist development and brings in its wake institutional changes leading at first to a state of chronic depression, then to a monopolized economy in which profits are protected but human and material resources are persistently underutilized.

This condition of affairs in turn intensifies and sharpens a class struggle already implicit in the occupational division of society between business and industry. The logic of the referred-to 'struggle' pointed in Veblen's mind to a progressive undermining of the eighteenth century principles on which business enterprise rested, and ultimately to a socialist reconstruction of society. To this trend, however, as Paul Sweezy wrote, the vested interests would 'oppose a counterforce in the shape of aggressive national policies which, harnessing the people's fierce sense of nationalism, create illusion of a solidarity of national interests and impose on society the retrogressive discipline of the barracks and the police state'.[2]

1. *Ibid.*, pp. 36-37.
2. PAUL M. SWEEZY, 'Veblen on American Capitalism', in DOUGLAS F. DOWD, ed., *Thorstein Veblen: A Critical Reappraisal*, Ithaca, N. Y.: Cornell University Press, 1958, pp. 192-193.

Thus comes about the second aspect referred to above. In other words, in Veblen's mind the machine process pointed forward to socialism and national politics and backward to the militarization of society or even to barbarism. Neither, of course, would be compatible with business principles.

Veblen died in August 1929, and he did not live to see the coming of the Great Depression or the surge of the *National Socialist* movement in Germany. But it would have been interesting if he had lived for four more years!

In the end, Veblen did not venture to predict anything definite for the future of American capitalism; but, according to Joseph Dorfman, a few months before his death he is said to have stated that the best hope he saw were the Communists.[1]

Schumpeter characterized Veblen as a sociologist. But Charles Schultze, a senior fellow at the Brookings Institution and a recent president of the American Economic Association said: 'When you dig deep down, economists are scared to death of being sociologists'.[2] This may explain the latter-day alienation which Veblen suffers in the dominant circle of academic economists in America.

1. JOSEPH DORFMAN, *Thorstein Veblen and His America*, New York: The Viking Press, 1934, p. 500.
2. ROBERT KUTTNER, 'The Poverty of Economics', p. 76.

CHAPTER FIVE
Modern Institutionalism

In summarizing the chronological tree of institutional economists, Allan Gruchy wrote:

> Although there has been some overlapping of generations of institutionalists, one can discern three well-defined periods in the development of institutional economic thought. The first period is associated with Thorstein Veblen's work, which was done in the years 1890-1925. The second period includes institutionalists such as Wesley C. Mitchell, John R. Commons, and John M. Clark who came after Veblen and worked during the years 1925-1939. The third or current period is that of the present-day institutionalists such as John K. Galbraith, Clarence E. Ayres, and Gunnar Myrdal whose contributions to institutional economics have been made primarily since 1939.[1]

One can immediately see in the above mentioned group of economists that there is nothing like sectarian homogeneity which usually characterizes a particular school of economists. This is perhaps because institutional economists, all of them, emphasize open models in their methodological approach-models which do not exclude any fresh orientation in different directions.

Besides, Veblen, from whom the institutional school is said to have started, was in many ways an eccentric man. Although he displayed flashes of insight which opened the minds of his colleagues and students to new ways of thinking on sundry matters of our society, it was difficult to obtain a systematic picture of his doctrine from his lectures or conversations. Temperamentally he was not eager to have himself understood. Furthermore, Veblen, during his academic life, moved from one place to another and did not have the chance to plant his roots so to speak, in the academic soil, where it would have been conducive to cultivating a coterie of his disciples.

Take the case of Wesley Mitchell, who both subjectively and

---

1. ALLAN G. GRUCHY, 'Institutional Economics: Its Development and Prospects', 1977, p. 11.

objectively was one of the closest disciples of Veblen. It has been acknowledged that 'Veblen's influence on him was profound';[1] and 'Mitchell appears to have been jarred out of whatever predilections he may have held for classical or neoclassical economic theory by Veblen's essays near the turn of the century. He was impressed by the view that economics must approach its problems from the evolutionary point of view, and by the idea that the key to an adequate understanding of the working of the economic system must rest upon an understanding of the human habits of thought and institutions which direct economic activity'.[2] But it must be admitted that although Mitchell 'delighted in Veblen's play of ideas, and upsetting of revealed orthodoxies, he departed from Veblen's type of study or at least went beyond it, in so far as Veblen was content to stand orthodoxy on its head, and to offer brilliant heretical insights, without undergoing the labor of systematic verification, and especially of measurement. These last areas were Mitchell's intellectual passion'.[3] And probably Homan was right in saying that 'it is not a little curious that the most eminent of our economic workmen in the field of minute analysis of statistical data should be so heavily indebted to an impressionistic cosmic philosopher like Veblen, who heroically distorts facts and shows no evidence of commerce with figures'.[4] But again, Milton Friedman may also be right in saying that 'I am inclined to believe that Mitchell's conception of the business cycle as a self-generating process is ultimately traceable to the influence of Thorstein Veblen, less, however, through Veblen's cycle theory than through his emphasis on the importance of studying the evolution of institutions and his conception of economic history as a process of "cumulative change" in which one phase of historical development can be

1. FREDERICK C. MILLS, 'A Professional Sketch', in *Wesley Clair Mitchell – The Economic Scientist*, edited by ARTHUR F. BURNS, New York: National Bureau of Economic Research, 1952, p. 109.

2. PAUL T. HOMAN, 'Place in Contemporary Economic Thought', in *Wesley Clair Mitchell – The Economic Scientist*, ed by ARTHUR F. BURNS, pp. 161-162.

3. JOHN MAURICE CLARK, 'Memorial Address', in *Wesley Clair Mitchell – The Economic Scientist*, ed. by ARTHUR F. BURNS, p. 142.

4. PAUL T. HOMAN, 'Place in Contemporany Economic Thought', p. 192.

understood only in terms of the conditions out of which it grew and itself becomes the source of further change'.[1]

One can see from these accounts how even the most direct successor of Veblen is related only in a limited fashion to the mentor's teachings. Other economists who are classified as institutionalists are also unique in their ways; but there are still certain common characteristics which, if loosely, bind them together.

What, then, are the elements which ally them in the same camp? We may summarize them under the following four headings: (1) the emphasis on the *open-system* character of production and consumption, thus a broader view of the scope of economics; (2) an interest in the *evolutionary* course along which the industrial economies are moving, with emphasis on the dynamic process of *technological change* and *circular cumulative causation*; (3) awareness of a growing need for guidance that can be supplied only through some form of overall social management of *planning*; and, finally, (4) recognition that economics must become a *normative* science, positively formulating social goals and objectives.

For the purpose of illustrating modern institutionalism in the above sense, we may draw upon the examples of Gunnar Myrdal (1898-1987),[2] John Kenneth Galbraith (1908) and William K. Kapp (1910-1976). All three economists echoed the warning that conventional mainstream economics was no longer able to meet the requirements for an effective tool of analysis for the problems with which modern society is confronted. Myrdal spoke, in the American Economic Association meeting of December 1971, that 'economic science is in a serious crisis, in my view very much more revolutionary for our research approaches than was the Keynesian revolution three decades ago'.[3] Galbraith referred to the situation as the 'disconcerting obsolescence in the profession of economics', which was due to the fact that 'economics be-

1. Milton Friedman, 'The Economic Theorist', in *Wesley Clair Mitchell – The Economic Scientist*, p. 256.

2. Although these lectures were presented in 1985, Gunnar Myrdal's death preceded their publication.

3. Gunnar Myrdal, 'Response to Introduction', *The American Economic Review*, May 1972, p. 461.

comes progressively more inadequate as a basis for social judgment and as a guide to public policy'.[1] Kapp, too, made a similar point by describing the traditional doctrine as a case of 'conceptual freeze' and predicted that 'it is not unlikely that this freeze will be broken in the calculable future under the impact of new facts, new evidence of environmental disruption, new catastrophes and an increasing public opposition to the deterioration of the physical and social environment'.[2]

This last point of Kapp's was repeatedly emphasized by Myrdal as he said: 'a crisis and the ensuing alteration of research approaches are not simply an autonomous development of our science but are mostly caused by the external forces of change in the society we are studying and living in as participants'.[3] As a matter of fact, Myrdal confesses that when he 'first came to America at the very end of the 1920s . . . the "wind of the future" was institutional economics . . . At that time I was utterly critical of this new orientation of economics. I was in the "theoretical" stage of my personal development as an economist. I even had something to do with the initiation of the Econometric Society, which was planned as a defense organization against the institutionalists'.[4] However, as Myrdal came to be involved in social equality problems in Sweden especially after a Labor Government came into power in 1932, he found that these types of problems could not be handled scientifically except by broadening the approach to all human relations. And when subsequently (in 1938) he accepted responsibility for a study of race relations in America, he found himself writing a book about the entire American civilization. 'From then on', as he writes, 'more definitely I came to see that in reality there are no economic, sociological, psychological problems, but just problems and they are all mixed and composite. In research, the only permissible demarcation is between relevant and irrelevant conditions. The

1. JOHN KENNETH GALBRAITH, *The New Industrial State*, Boston: Houghton Mifflin, 1967, pp. 407-408.

2. K. WILLIAM KAPP, 'The Open-System Character of the Economy and Its Implications', in *Economics in the Future: Towards a New Paradigm*, edited by KURT DOPFER, London: Macmillan, 1976, p. 105.

3. GUNNAR MYRDAL, 'Response to Introduction', p. 456.

4. *Ibid.*, p. 457.

problems are regularly also political and have moreover to be seen in historical perspective'.[1] That is to say, words, again in his own words, 'Through the type of problems I came to deal with, I became an institutional economist after having been in my early youth one of the most ardent "theoretical" economists'.[2] And he later argues that 'we are going to see a rapid development of economic science in the institutional direction and that much which is now hailed as most sophisticated theory will in hindsight be seen to have been a temporary aberration into superficiality and irrelevance'.[3] Institutional economics is destined to be winning ground at the expense of conventional economics, according to Myrdal, not only because of the strength of its logic, but also 'because a broader approach will be needed for dealing in an effective way with the practical and political problems that are now towering and threatening to overwhelm us'.[4]

Myrdal had established himself as a first-rate economist already by the beginning of the 1930s through the publication of *The Political Element in the Development of Economic Theory*.[5] There are two other publications by him during the period up until 1932, when he considered himself a 'theorist'. One, *The Problem of Price Formation* (available in Swedish only), was published in 1927; and the other, *Monetary Equilibrium* (for which both German and English translations exist) came out in 1931.

As stated earlier, Myrdal moved gradually toward institutional economics after 1932; and by the time he wrote 'Preface to the English Edition' of *The Political Element* book in 1953, he identified in his own words the basic weakness of his earlier work as follows:

Throughout the book there lurks the idea that when all metaphysical elements are radically cut away, a healthy body of positive eco-

1. GUNNAR MYRDAL, 'Institutional Economics', a lecture of the University of Wisconsin, December 15, 1977, reprinted in Gunnar Myrdal, *Essays and Lectures After 1975*, Kyoto: Keibunsha, 1979, p. 106.

2. GUNNAR MYRDAL, 'Response to Introduction', p. 459.

3. *Ibid.*, p. 459.

4. GUNNAR MYRDAL, *Essays and Lectures After 1975*, p. 112.

5. The original Swedish edition came out in 1930, with the German edition in 1932 and the Engtish translation in 1953. A new Swedish edition appeared in 1972 with a lengthy special preface by the author.

CHAPTER FIVE

nomic theory will remain, which is altogether independent of valuations. Political conclusions can then be inferred simply by adding to the objective scientific knowledge of the facts a chosen set of value premises.

This implicit belief in the existence of a body of scientific knowledge acquired independently of all valuations is, as I now see it, naive empiricism . . . Valuations are necessarily involved already at the stage when we observe facts and carry on theoretical analysis, and not only at the stage when we draw political inferences from facts and valuations.

I have therefore arrived at the belief in the necessity of working always, from the beginning to the end, with explicit value premises.[1]

Now that Myrdal came to be convinced that economics had to be a 'moral science' and could not shirk the issue of valuations, he had to answer the question of what comes first in the bill of particulars demanding the attention of economists. He had no hesitation in replying to this query by highlighting the importance of the *equality* issue. When addressing the American Economic Association meeting in 1971, he remarked 'A basic deficiency in the writings of economists in the establishment school is their playing down of the equality issue . . . In regard to the study of development in underdeveloped countries, we are now in a period of transition . . . The new approach will be institutional, focusing on the equality issue and taking into due account social and economic stratification, the political forces anchored in these institutions and in peoples' attitudes, and the productivity consequences when levels of living are extremely low'.[2]

Appropriately enough, Myrdal developed this idea more extensively in the subsequent years, culminating in his Nobel Memorial Lecture (March 17, 1975) after he received the Nobel Economics Prize in December 1974. This lecture was entitled: 'The Equality Issue in World Development'; and it gave an admirable summary of his basic view as an institutional economist, in particular as regards what should be done to cope with the

1. GUNNAR MYRDAL, *The Political Element in the Development of Economic Theory*, translated by PAUL STREETEN, London: Routledge and Kegan Paul, 1953, pp. VII-VIII.
2. GUNNAR MYRDAL, 'Response to Introduction', p. 460.

aggravating inequality in the international scene. He cited in this lecture the problems of population explosion and of depletion of nonrenewable resources, along with the food crisis, as factors involved in circular causation with cumulative effects – a typical institutional approach, one may say. And he formulated his prescription for developing countries as follows:

What they do need is fundamental changes in the conditions under which they are living and working. The important thing is that these changes regularly imply both greater equality and increased productivity at the same time. The two purposes are inextricably joined, much more, in fact, than in developed countries. To these imperatively needed radical changes belong, first, land reform, but also a fundamental redirection of education and health work.[1]

There is little question that J. K. Galbraith qualifies as a modern institutional economist. He himself wrote:

Veblen was perhaps dangerously attractive to someone of my background . . . Veblen's scholarship was an eruption against all who, in consequence of wealth, occupation, ethnic origin or elegance of manner, made invidious claim (a Veblen phrase) to superior worldly position. I knew the mood.[2]

However, Galbraith was of the opinion that 'Veblen was not a constructive figure; no alternative economics system and no penetrating reforms are associated with his name. There was danger here. Veblen was a skeptic and an enemy of pretense. Those who drank too deeply could be in doubt about everything and everybody; they could believe that all effort at reform was humbug. I've sought to resist this tendency'.[3] And indeed, he did. As Arthur Schlesinger, Jr. wrote, 'What is salient from the viewpoint of political economy is the skill with which Galbraith brought institutionalism to bear on public policy. A political leader could steep himself in Veblen, Patten, Commons, Mitchell, Ayres and other notable institutionalists without gaining much enlightenment about specific policy decisions; what to

1. GUNNAR MYRDAL, *Essays and Lectures After 1975*, p. 19.
2. JOHN KENNETH GALBRAITH, *A Life in Our Times*, London: André Deutsch Ltd., 1981, p. 30.
3. *Ibid.*, p. 30.

do with the budget, interest rates, exchange convertibility, tariffs and son on . . . Galbraith [on the other hand] was especially qualified to unite institutionalism with dynamic equilibrium analysis; to marry, so to speak, Veblen and Keynes. The result was an institutionalist model that could deliver policy choices'.[1]

Of the four characteristic strands of institutionalism mentioned earlier, Galbraith shares all of them, though in differing fullness. Before he launched upon his famed trilogy (*The Affluent Society*, 1958, *The New Industrial State*, 1967, and *Economics and Public Purpose*, 1973), he proposed the concept of 'countervailing power' in his analysis of American capitalism[2] – the concept which clearly goes beyond the closed-system character of neoclassical economics. The concept of 'dependence effect' is also an example of the open-system character of consumption where the consumers' sovereignty is circumscribed by the aggressive policies of suppliers.

In addition, on the role which technology plays in the evolutionary process of modern economies, Galbraith made a telling point that 'the enemy of the market is not ideology but the engineer',[3] and he developed the theme of the imperatives of technology under six headings, as follows:

First. An increasing span of time separates the beginning from the completion of any task . . . The more thoroughgoing the application of technology – in common or at least frequent language, the more sophisticated the production process – the farther back the application of knowledge will be carried. The longer, accordingly, will be the time between the initiation and completion of the task . . .

Second. There is an increase in the capital that is committed to production aside from that occasioned by increased output. The increased time, and therewith the increased investment in goods in process costs money. So does the knowledge which is applied to the various elements of the task . . .

Third. With increasing technology the commitment of time and

1. ARTHUR SCHLESINGER Jr., 'The Political Galbraith', *The Journal of Post-Keynesian Economics*, Fall 1984, pp. 10-11.
2. JOHN KENNETH GALBRAITH, *American Capitalism: The Concept of Countervailing Power*, Boston: Houghton Mifflin, 1952.
3. JOHN KENNETH GALBRAITH, *The New Industrial State*, p. 32.

money tends to be made ever more inflexibly to the performance of a particular task. That task must be precisely defined before it is divided and subdivided into its component parts . . .

Fourth. Technology requires specialized manpower. This will be evident. Organized knowledge can be brought to bear, not surprisingly, only by those who possess it . . .

Fifth. The inevitable counterpart of specialization is organization. This is what brings the work of specialists to a coherent result . . . So complex, indeed, will be the job of organizing specialists that there will be specialists on organization . . .

Sixth. From the time and capital that must be committed, the inflexibility of this commitment, the needs of large organization and the problems of market performance under conditions of advanced technology, comes the necessity for planning.[1]

Thus we are led to the third characteristic strand of institutionalism, i.e., the problem of planning, not only as an inevitable concomitant of technological progress for modern business firms on the forefront but also for the economy as a whole. On this latter point, another typical Galbraithian terminology came into vogue, i.e., 'social imbalance'. According to his own words; 'The line which divides our area of wealth from our area of poverty is roughly that which divides privately produced and marketed goods and services from publicly rendered services. Our wealth in the first is not only in startling contrast with the meagerness of the latter but our wealth in privately produced goods is, to a marked degree, the cause of crisis in the supply of public services. For we have failed to see the importance, indeed the urgent need, of maintaining a balance between the two.'[2]

Thus we have the undeniable condition of 'social imbalance', recognition of which comes from Galbraith's institutionalist inference that the market mechanism by itself does not 'deliver the goods', so to speak, with the normative criterion of social goals and objectives demands. This, incidentally, is the fourth strand of institutional economics mentioned earlier. Galbraith's concern

1. *Ibid.*, p. 13-16.
2. JOHN KENNETH GALBRAITH, *The Affluent Society*, Boston: Houghton Mifflin, 1958, p. 195.

with this aspect led him to *The Nature of Mass Poverty*,[1] in which he developed the theme of 'the equilibrium of poverty' evoking an explanatory tool of circular causation – a methodology common with Myrdal.

Let us, then, turn to Kapp whose conversion to institutional economics was quite early. Already in his doctoral dissertation,[2] which he wrote in his formative years as an economist, Kapp pointed out the importance of *how we posed* the question of cost. Traditional economic theory posed the question of 'what is the cost of public policy'; but Kapp held that the question we should pose was: 'What is the social cost attendant to the situation where government leaves the economy in the condition of *laissez-faire*?'. He carried on his research with keen awareness of the importance of this problem of social cost and produced his *opus*: *The Social Costs of Private Enterprise* (1950) which was later revised with a new title of *The Social Cost of Business Enterprise* (1963).

Thus it was natural for him to be concerned with the problem of environmental spillover effects. It is well-known that Pigou popularized the concept of externalities, arguing for government action in correcting for undesirable external effects. Kapp deals with a similar problem, but he objects to the use of such terms as 'externalities' on the grounds that such a term implies the closed-system character of the economy. Pollution of air, for example, may be 'external' to business enterprises, but should be considered, according to Kapp, 'internal' to the economy as a whole and should be dealt with as such. In other words, Kapp shares with other institutional economists the methodological precept of the *open-system* character of the economy.[3] He was more conscious of this need than either Myrdal or Galbraith since the major concern throughout his life was the fight against environmental disruption.

1. JOHN KENNETH GALBRAITH, *The Nature of Mass Poverty*, Cambridge, Mass.: Harvard University Press, 1979.

2. WILLIAM K. KAPP, *Planwirtschaft und Aussenhandel*, Geneva: Geory et Cie, S. A. Librairie de l'Université, 1936.

3. WILLIAM K. KAPP, *Towards a Science of Man in Society*, The Hague: M. Nijlioff, 1961.

It was again natural for him to emphasize the *normative* character of economic science – the fourth of the institutionalist strands mentioned earlier. As he wrote:

As soon as the open character of economic systems is fully realised the formulation of social goals and objectives and the problem of collective choices can no longer be avoided. Such objectives and choices with respect to the maintenance of dynamic states of ecological and economic balance essential for the maintenance and improvement of the conditions of social and individual existence (quality of life) must become the point of departure for a normative science of economics.[1]

In more concrete terms, 'what is required is to overcome the essentially dualistic conceptualisation of economy and environment in order to give our analysis the necessary empirical content. Determination of basic needs and requirements of health and survival, of environmental norms and maximum tolerable levels of contamination; environmental-impact studies of alternative technologies in specific localities rather than linear physical flow models are some of the empirical and quantitative problems that call for exploration and analysis; social science will have to come to terms with the key problem of the open-system character of the economy – the fact, namely, that production derives material inputs from the physical and decisive impulses from the social system which, in turn, may be disrupted and disorganised by the emission of residual wastes up to a point where social reproduction itself may be threatened'.[2]

At almost every one of the international conferences where environmental disruption was discussed, Kapp was an indispensable participant; and when the International Social Science Council organized a symposium of social scientists to discuss that problem in Tokyo in 1970, preliminary to the Stockholm Conference on Human Environment of 1972, Kapp played a leading role in drafting the 'Tokyo Resolution' in which it was stated:

1. WILLIAM K. KAPP, 'The Open-System Character of the Economy and Its Implications', in *Economics in the Future*: Towards a Nero Paradigm, edited by KURT DOPFER, London, Macmillan, p. 1976, p. 101.
2. *Ibid.*, p. 98.

Above all, it is important that we urge the adoption in law of the principle that every person is entitled by right to the environment free of elements which infringe human health and well-being and the nature's endowment, including its beauty, which shall be the heritage of the present to the future generations.[1]

Kapp continued to concentrate his energy on this environmental issue until his premature death by heart attack while attending the Inter-University Center Conference on environmental problems in Dubrovnik, Yugoslavia, in April 1976.

It may be appropriate to conclude this chapter by quoting a paragraph from Galbraith's latest book as representing the well-nigh common opinion shared by institutional economists today:

The separation of economics from politics and political motivation is a sterile thing. It is also a cover for the reality of economic power and motivation. And it is a prime source of misjudgment and error in economic policy. No volume on the history of economics can conclude without the hope that the subject will be reunited with politics to form again the larger discipline of political economy.[2]

1. SHIGETO TSURU, ed., *Proceedings of International Symposium on Environmental Disruption: A Challenge to Social Scientists*, Tokyo: International Social Science Council, 1970, pp. 319-320.

2. JOHN KENNETH GALBRAITH, *Economics in Perspective: A Critical History*, Boston: Houghton Mifflin, 1987, p. 299.

CHAPTER SIX
The Future of Institutional Economics I:
In Place of GNP

Is there a future for institutional economics? Myrdal is confident that there is, as he wrote:

'I foresee that within the next ten or twenty years the now fashionable highly abstract analysis of conventional economists will lose out. Though its logical basis is weak – it is founded on utterly unrealistic, poorly scrutinised, and rarely even explicitly stated assumptions – its decline will be mainly an outcome of tremendous changes which, with crushing weight, are falling upon us'.[1]

I am inclined to agree with him. Firstly, in contrast to the somewhat imperious attitude of abstract economic theorists typified by John Eatwell's remark to the effect that 'if the world is not like the model, so much the worse for the world',[2] institutional economists set store, above all, on the empirical studies of the subject matter – our society in its manifold aspects – which undergoes evolutionary changes in the course of historical development. In a sense, most typical in this respect was Wesley Mitchell, about whom Albert B. Wolfe wrote:

Mitchell's Veblenian institutionalism seems to boil down to substantially this: that men in the mass, at any given time and in any given culture-complex, behave in certain standardized ways, according to uniform but not simple patterns; these patterns undergo an evolutionary drift which can be roughly measured by the statistical device of time series and which with adequate empirical analysis is amenable to some degree of rational control and direction.[3]

As a matter of fact, Mitchell was one of those economists who held, on the basis of thoroughgoing empirical studies, that busi-

1. GUNNAR MYRDAL, 'The Meaning and Validity of Institutional Economics', in *Economics in the Future: Towards a New Paradigm*, ed. by KURT DOPFER, London; Macmillan, 1976, p. 86.
2. Quoted in ROBERT KUTTNER, 'The Poverty of Economics', *The Atlantic Monthly*, February 1985.
3. ALBERT B. WOLFE, 'Views on the Scope and Methods of Economics', in WESLEY CLAIR MITCHELL: *The Economic Scientist*, cit., p. 212.

ness cycles punctuated by crises are phenomena related somehow to the economic system which we call capitalism. Thus he wrote:

> Business cycles do not become a prominent feature of economic experience in any community until a large proportion of its members have begun to live by making and spending money incomes. On the other hand, such cycles seem to appear in all countries when economic activity becomes organized predominantly in this fashion. These observations suggest that there is an organic connection between that elaborate form of economic organization which we may call 'business economy,' and recurrent cycles of prosperity and depression.[1]

Stimulated by Mitchell and others, the discipline of economics became highly empiricism-conscious in the decade of 1920s. This was further abetted by the flowering of macroeconomics in the wake of the Keynesian revolution. Although it was two centuries ago that Edmund Burke wrote: 'the age of chivalry is gone; that of sophisters, economists, and calculators has succeeded', it may be more appropriate for Burke's remark to be applied to the past half century of statistical deluge. In particular, concepts like GNP, once reserved for technical textbooks only, have become even household words, as well as customary usage in daily papers and parliamentary discussions.

Although Mitchell is classified as an institutional economist, he did not share as much as others in the school the need to recognize that economics had to become a normative science, positively formulating social goals and objectives. He preferred to let 'the facts speak by themselves'. Here, however, arises a difficulty. Mitchell might have warned against the welfare connotation; but there has been a persistent tendency among publicists and even among some economists to consider the per capita real GNP as an approximation to the average welfare of a nation and to view its growth as a boon. Most institutional economists have been critical of this tendency. For example, Myrdal wrote:

> Our politicians, of all political parties, stick to the inept concept of 'growth' which is embodied in the gross national product or one

---

1. WESLEY MITCHELL, *Business Cycles. The Problem and Its Setting*, New York: National Bureau of Economic Research, 1927, p. 182.

of its derivatives. We economists, by not having scrutinized more intensively that even statistically rather spurious concept, and by ourselves commonly utilizing 'growth' in that sense uncritically as a main value premise in our discussions of practical economic policy, have unfortunately contributed to restricting the mental horizon of politicians and of the common people.[1]

Economists' habit of equating the growth of GNP with that of economic welfare used to be firmly enough grounded. There was a time, for one thing, when mass unemployment was a direct cause of severe suffering for millions of people and any measure that expanded effective demand, even including the non-sensical digging and refilling of holes in the ground, was regarded as a positive step toward increasing welfare so long as it brought about a net increase in employment. In fact, the close association of growth in GNP with that of economic welfare, in the minds of economists, developed in the period immediately following the Great Depression, thanks largely to the Keynesian revolution in economic thinking.

But aside from this short-run policy orientation of the GNP concept, there is a longer-range association, which could be predicated, between the size of GNP and the magnitude of economic welfare provided certain assumptions could be justified. The assumptions are of the type inherent in a mature exchange economy where practically all economic goods are priced in the market. They include: (1) that external effects, either positive or negative, are insignificant; (2) that the condition of consumer sovereignty obtains; and (3) that the failure of the reward system, for whatever reason, is insignificant.

Even in the heyday of competitive capitalism these three assumptions could not be fully justified. Negative external effects were often serious enough. But in the era when the minimum requirements for the health of the workers were ignored in the interest of industrial prosperity, environmental disamenities were of secondary consideration. The doctrine of consumer sovereignty, too, one may say, was never more than a complacent rational-

1. GUNNAR MYRDAL, 'Institutional Economies', a lecture at the University of Winsconsin, December 15, 1977, *cit.*, p. 15.

ization by economists. In an address to manufacturers, John Ruskin perorated, more than one hundred years ago.[1]

> You must remember always that your business, as manufacturers, is to *form the market* as much as to supply it . . . But whatever happens to you, this, at least, is certain, that the whole of your life will have been spent in corrupting public taste and encouraging public extravagance. Every preference you have won by gaudiness must have been based on the purchaser's vanity; every demand you have created by novelty has fostered in the consumer a habit of discontent; and when you retire into inactive life, you may, as a subject of consolation for your declining years, reflect that precisely according to the extent of your past operations, your life has been successful in retarding the arts, tarnishing the virtues, and confusing the manners of your country.

Ruskin was no doubt a sensitive soul; but here is an insight — that 'manufacturers form the market' — which could not easily be refuted, even in the days of a laissez-faire market economy. As for the third assumption, it may be enough to make reference to the discriminating bias, due to inheritance, which gave a headstart to a select group of men, enabling them to capture a share in the national pie independently of their own efforts.

In spite of these deviations, however, we may say that, in the heyday of competitive capitalism, the presumption of a close association between magnitude of GNP and that of economic welfare was relatively free of seriously misleading connotations. But today matters are different in advanced capitalist societies. Not only is it true that technological progress has heightened the possibility of negative external effects of gigantic proportions, but at the same time the preference scale of consumers is gradually evolving in such a way that amenity rights of all kinds, not susceptible to quantification, are acquiring greater importance than before. It is especially important to remind ourselves at this point that nature, which is essentially a whole, made up of interrelated parts, best rewards those who respect this whole, and that as we make progress in the arts of controlling nature, the socio-economic system characterized by individualistic pur-

---

1. Lecture delivered at Bradford in March 1859. See JOHN RUSKIN, *The Two Paths*, London: Smith and Elder, 1859, pp. 109-110, italics added.

suit of profit maximization within the restricted horizon of 'internality' is less likely to be capable of coping with the task of making the best use of nature's endowments. Here, the term 'externality' is made to cover more and more of what, left out of the 'internal' calculation, is yet of increasing importance from the welfare point of view.

As for the presumption of consumer sovereignty, Ruskin's indictment would surprise no one today. Galbraith, in particular, made a similar point forcibly, and in a more matter-of-fact way, by contrasting the 'accepted sequence' of the unidirectional flow of instruction from consumer to market to producer with the 'revised sequence' where 'the producing firm reaches forward to control its markets and on beyond to manage the market behavior and shape the social attitude of those, ostensibly, that it serves'.[1] As regards the third assumption concerning the reward system, however, one could point to a kind of improvement in recent decades on the grounds that inheritance and gift taxes are severer today in most capitalist countries than before and, in addition, opportunity for higher education and training are undeniably greater now than in the last century. The principle of equal pay for equal work is also becoming a reality. But a question must be raised as to the meaningfulness of relating reward to the number of labor hours performed by each individual. We have already touched on this problem earlier and drawn attention to the fact that the degree of dependence, in the process of production, upon instruments incorporating man's 'universal productivity' is so large nowadays that human labor in its immediate form has ceased to be the great source of wealth, and labor time will cease to be the measure of wealth. We may be inexorably approaching the stage of social development where the precept of 'to each according to his needs and from each according to his ability' will apply. More important still, this very development demands that we revise our thinking on the significance of emphasizing flows, rather than stocks, when we wish to obtain a measure of economic welfare.

In other words, the close association which we could once

---

1. JOHN KENNETH GALBRAITH, *The New Industrial State*, p. 212.

assume between magnitude of GNP and that of economic welfare has become tenuous in advanced capitalist countries as the impact of technological progress upon productive relations renders the old assumptions increasingly untenable. Here again is the reason why the institutionalist orientation is destined to gain greater importance.

As stated earlier, the concept of GNP is predicated on the exchange of goods in the market, and is intended to cover those goods and services which are exchanged in the market. As a corollary of this, it may be added that the unit for measurement of GNP is money value as registered in the market. If one gram of opium, baneful as it may be, has the same market value as one kilogram of rice, these two items are considered equivalent in national income accounting. Welfare content is essentially concrete; but when aggregated into national income or GNP, all goods and services acquire a single dimension, namely that of market valuation, and the quantitative expression obtained does not necessarily relate to concrete welfare content.

Stated alternatively, the concept of GNP is best applicable to a mature market economy, and its welfare significance depends essentially upon the performance of markets as an objective intermediary between final consumers and suppliers. A viable market is a market which can be sustained by the 'money votes' of final consumers, who in turn part with such 'money votes' in order to satisfy their wants and needs. But here is the rub. Man's needs in a society are often relative to institutional and other conditions of that society which may be contrived; and man's wants are often artificially stimulated by suppliers of goods and services who, in extreme cases, are capable of actually embracing the market under their wings. In other words, among the 'money votes' which consumers cast, and which thus enter as components into GNP, there are some components whose welfare significance are questionable; and here we shall classify them into five different types:

1. 'the cost of life' type;
2. 'interference of income' type;
3. 'the institutionalization of waste' type;

4. depletion of social wealth;
5. inefficiency of dynamic adjustment.

1. 'The Cost of Life'

We are all aware that, within our own consumption expenditure, there are certain items which fall into the category of necessary costs, which we prefer would remain as small as possible. Heating cost in a cold country is the simplest example. High commuting cost without compensating advantages in environmental amenities, as we observe in a dense urban sprawl such as Tokyo, is another. But there are more sophisticated examples of cost-type consumption which induce citizens to part with their 'money votes' on account of certain institutional and social developments. One example of this kind relates to the widespread use nowadays of expensive burglar alarms in America to cope with the mounting incidence of burglary in homes. A news item in *The New York Times*,[1] with the headline 'Booming Burglar Alarm Industry Finds That Fear of Crime Pays' reported:

Sales, they (manufacturers of burglar alarms) say, are a direct reflection of rising crime rates, and the projections are for a continuing steep upward trend. Burglary, or unlawful entry to commit a felony, was the single most frequently committed crime last year (1969), with 81 percent of the incidents listed as unsolved. Homes and apartments are prime targets. In Los Angeles, the city with the highest crime rate in the nation, the police reported 65,546 burglaries and attempts last year, against 36,256 in 1960. Single residences led the list with 21,968 burglaries, and apartments were second with 14,092 . . . A typical home alarm system protects all exterior doors and windows with contact switches or other circuit interrupters. Entry when the system is not deactivated with a key or a switch usually sounds an alarm, or turns on the lights, or both. In some systems, it also alerts the installing company's central headquarters, which in turn calls the police . . . Such a system costs about $500 to install with a service charge of about $20 to $30 a month.

Whatever the explanation for the prevalence of this type of crime, citizens are more or less forced to take self-protecting measures on an individualistic basis. The cost of burglar alarms

1. *The New York Times*, August 16, 1970, 'Booming Burglar Alarm Industry Finds That Fear of Crime Pays'.

for homes is part of consumer expenditure, and thus constitutes a component of GNP. However, it is clearly what might be called a 'cost type' consumption, or a part of 'the cost of life', and no one would dispute the fact that the smaller it is, the better.

While true that it is often very difficult to draw a hard and fast line between cost-type and end-object type consumption, there are fairly clear-cut cases of formerly luxury or semi-luxury items becoming necessities in a dynamic situation. A good example, from Japan, would be the process of disappearance of public bath-houses. At present, about one-third of the population of Tokyo ward districts have no private baths in their homes, and there are upwards of 2,000 public bath-houses in the area. The break-even point for a typical public bath-house calls for about 600 daily customers; and yet it is reported that customers of many bath-houses have dropped to one-half of this level, owing to the steady increase of private baths at home. Thus, one after another, the public bath-houses are closing; and casualities in recent years have been at a rate of twenty per year. Rates are periodical-ly raised, but the loss of customers proves fatal for many. When a public bath-house disappears in a typical district, one third of the residents must choose between two alternatives: either going to a bath-house farther away or installing a private bath at home. Private baths may be referred to as a semi-luxury; but under the circumstances they *become a necessity*. Furthermore, when one public bath-house disappears, the range of consumers' choice is narrowed.

A similar problem arises whenever a public establishment re-quiring a fair number of customers to break even competes with private means of satisfying the same need on an individual basis. A bus line may be discontinued at a stage where there are still a large number of people for whom it is indispensable. When that happens, the purchase of motorcyles or automobiles becomes a necessity and people may well consider such an expenditure as an added cost of life.

2. 'Interference of Income'

The term was used originally by the late Schumpeter who, in the light mood of cocktail conversation, jestingly disparaged the profession of American lawyers on whose services he had to depend when he went through the red tape of naturalization. Keynes, no doubt, would have sympathized with him for he, too, apparently felt the ubiquity of lawyers in the United States as essentially redundant. The story he told in his closing speech at the Bretton Woods Conference is quite well known.[1]

The 'interference of income' phenomenon might be defined as the generation of income by otherwise dispensable services, which are made indispensable through built-in institutional arrangements in the society concerned. There is usually a historical background explaining why a particular service acquires built-in indispensability in a particular society, and there is, of course, no opprobrium implied in singling out a particular profession as 'income-interfering'. As a matter of fact, an 'income-interfering' profession in a particular society draws very often the best of brains in that society and its members distinguish themselves as outstanding citizens of the community. If lawyers serve as an example of 'interference of income' in the United States, we may say that bankers and real estate dealers do so in Japan.

Here we may append a concrete example of the role of legal specialists citing a recent news item from the United States. With a headline: 'Lawyers Stand to Reap Substantial Rewards in Penn Central Case', *The Wall Street Journal* reported:[2]

> To creditors, shareholders and bondholders of Penn Central Transportation Co., the railroad's decision to reorganize under the Federal Bankruptcy Act means plenty of uncertainty and woe. But for many members of the legal profession, it's nothing short of a bonanza ... By the estimate of one attorney familiar with the intricacies of railroad reorganization, about 1,000 lawyers could eventually become involv-

---

1. Here is the relevant passage as reproduced in ROY FORBES HARROD, *The Life of John Maynard Keynes*, London: Macmillan, 1951, p. 583: 'I have been known to complain that, to judge from results in this lawyer-ridden land, the *Mayflower*, when she sailed from Plymouth, must have been entirely filled with lawyers. When I first visited Mr. Morgenthau in Washington some three years ago accompanied only by my secretary, the boys in your Treasury curiously enquired of him – where is your lawyer? When it was explained that I had none – "Who then does your thinking for you?" was the rejoinder'.

2. *The Wall Street Journal*, July 23, 1970, 'Lawyers Stand to Reap Substantial Rewards in Penn Central Case'.

ed, drawing fees totalling as much as $50 million. 'And that', the lawyer adds, 'could be a low figure' . . . In any event, some lawyers could well make an entire career out of the Penn Central mess. The late Russell Dearmont was appointed counsel to the trustee of the Missouri Pacific shortly after it entered reorganization proceedings in 1934. The case dragged on until 1956. Soon afterward, Mr. Dearmont was named a vice president of the road. He moved up to president in 1957.

The pattern of Mr. Dearmont's career is strikingly similar to that of many a banker in Japan.

3. 'The Institutionalization of Waste'

Veblen, as early as 1904,[1] wrote, and I quote:

> The absorption of goods and services by extra-industrial expenditures, expenditures which, seen from the standpoint of industry, are pure waste, would have to go on in an increasing volume. If the wasteful expenditure slackens, the logical outcome should be a considerable perturbation of business and industry, followed by depression.

This is a prophetic statement; but it is misleading to refer to these wasteful expenditures as 'expenditures which, seen from the standpoint of industry, are pure waste'. Business enterprises by nature abhor waste in the context of their own calculations. Whether a certain good or service is wasteful or not is not to be judged 'from the standpoint of industry' but only from the standpoint of final consumers. What is at issue here, however, is not a moralistic assessment of extravagance or dissipation. Economists *qua* economists have nothing to say to a person who knowingly wastes something for his own enjoyment. But when waste is institutionalized in such a way that a less wasteful alternative, which may well be preferred by consumers, is deliberately withheld from the market, we are called upon to analyze the mechanism which makes this possible, and to draw out the necessary implications for economic welfare. Examples of built-in obsolescence, etc., are legion, as popularized by the writings of Vance Packard, and the mechanism which

---

1. THORSTEIN VEBLEN, *The Theory of Business Enterprise*, p. 120.

encourages this type of GNP-inflating expenditure has been fully analyzed by Galbraith.

4. Depletion of Social Wealth

GNP is a flow in the same way as my monthly expenditure or daily food intake is a flow. Just as I can increase my monthly expenditure by drawing upon my past savings, we can make our GNP larger than otherwise would be the case by depleting our store of resources without replacing them.

It is true that there are certain resources used in the process of production that cannot be replaced. The earth's mineral deposits are of this type. As far as these resources are concerned, it would be meaningless to speak of replacing them, and the only alternative open to us is to find ways of economizing on their use when the depletion process goes too far. There are, however, various other types of social wealth which, to different degrees and with differing time patterns, can be replaced after use. Forestry and marine resources come immediately to mind in this respect, but we may also include here clean water, natural beauty, and other environmental endowments, all of which, after all, provide a source to a healthy and enjoyable life. By ignoring the need for conserving such amenities, a country can raise the growth rate of its GNP more rapidly than if it paid heed to them. The rapid growth of Japan's economy during the last decade provides a good example of this.

5. Inefficiency of Dynamic Adjustment

An economy in the modern world is always confronted with the need for dynamic adjustment in its use of resources. An example may be drawn from present-day Japan, where the area traditionally under rice cultivation is now patently in excess of needs and is likely to remain so in the foreseeable future, although transfer of land to other uses is called for to the extent of at least 500,000 acres. In fact, as many as 830,000 acres of paddy fields were left idle in 1970 and compensation was paid to farmers who cooperated in this reduction program. In the coming year, an even larger area is likely to be involved in this program.

93

There is a pressing need for land both for industrial sites and for residential quarters. The need for additional factory sites by 1975, for example, was estimated to be about 250,000 acres, as calculated on the basis of the 10.6 percent per annum GNP growth rate during 1971-1975. The recent economic growth of Japan has seen a radical shift in the industrial structure – a shift from primary to secondary industries with greater and greater concentration in the heavy and engineering branches of manufacturing. Probable development in the near future is also in the same direction. If such is the case, we may expect that reallocation of land use from rice cultivation, for example, to factory sites, would be in order, and would continue to be so in the near future. This is one type of dynamic adjustment which economic rationality calls for. Actual development, however, has been otherwise, not because rice land on the whole is inconveniently situated from the standpoint of locating manufacturing plants, but for a number of reasons, among which the subsidy and compensation programs for farmers and the farmers' expectation (thus far justified) of a continued rise in land prices have been major factors holding in check any large-scale reallocation program. As a matter of fact, the cost of reclaiming coastal bays is now definitely lower than the price demanded by farmers for nearby agricultural land for potential non-agricultural use. Thus the government, in cooperation with prefectural authorities, who generally welcome the establishment of new industries in their regions, has started a gigantic reclamation program along almost the entire coast of Japan's archipelago. The program for 1966-1970 involved the creation of new factory sites by reclamation to the tune of 37,000 acres; and the five-year program for 1971-1975 was three times the size of this, the cost of which was expected to run to three trillion yen. This sum is equivalent, on an annual basis, to one half of the total value added in the iron and steel industry and will no doubt contribute to the growth of GNP to that extent. It may be added that reclamation, both in the recent past and as planned in the near future, is taking place in the coastal bay areas, many of which are included within national parks or government-designated parks, and is damaging not only to the natural beauty and to the recreational opportunities offered, but is also, in some places, crippling fishing industries unique to the region. The most flagrant instance of a national park being sacrificed for industrial expansion is the reclamation taking place in the Inland Sea. It is as if one were to spread the kitchen of one's house into the beautiful garden without providing for sewage facilities.

The unusually rapid growth of Japan's GNP during the past fifteen years can be shown to have entailed all five of the above-mentioned GNP-inflating factors. Those who are committed to 'growthmanship', when pressed on this point, do admit that some of the growth components of GNP have been of doubtful character from the welfare point of view, and that inefficiency in dynamic adjustment also existed. But, they point out, at least one thing is certain, namely, that the aggregate supply capacity of the country is indicated faithfully enough by the GNP index, and they go on to stress that given that capacity, which continues to grow, we can and should devise ways of improving our dynamic efficiency, and take measures to help restore consumer sovereignty to its rightful place.

Here is a problem which has been raised time and again in relation to the institutional motive force of economic activities under capitalism. An innocent GI was reported to have asked once: 'If our economy can prosper by the production of "the instruments of death", why could it not prosper better by the production of "the instruments of life"?'. On a more sophisticated level, Keynes himself deplored the fact, in 1940, that it might have well proved politically impossible, except in war time, to plan an expenditure program on a scale sufficient to confirm the validity of his new theory.[1] In other words, under given conditions of institutional arrangement, effective demand tends to flow in the directions circumscribed by the influence and resistance exercised by dominant interest groups in the society. Take the example of the reclamation project referred to in the previous paragraphs. Here is an industry, already established, doing business on a scale of 600 billion yen a year, obviously concerned with continuing in business. Pitched against them are individual

1. *New Republic*, July 29, 1940.

citizens, large in number but unorganized, who may deeply deplore the loss of environmental amenities but have no effective way of registering their 'money votes' in favor of conserving the beauty of nature, clean-water beaches, fishing facilities, etc. The only effective means they have at their disposal, at present, are political. Is economics incapable of translating the genuine preference of citizens in such matters as environmental amenities into terms comparable with those of market-valued goods and services so that it would somehow be possible to calculate the *net* positive welfare achieved? Must we visualize the situation as a confrontation between angel's and devil's advocates, neither of whom can concede to the other?

Attempts have been made in many quarters to compile some kind of a welfare index based on specific indicators, such as hospital beds, park areas, educational opportunities, sewage facilities, etc. Although each one of these is quantifiable, they are not commensurable in dollars and cents.

One need not dispute the usefulness of such a welfare index; but it certainly cannot take the place of GNP as an overall quantitative measure of economic welfare. A much more fruitful approach appears to me to be the resuscitation of Irving Fisher's concept of 'capital' and 'income'.[1] Attention was called to these concepts by Kenneth Boulding forty years ago.[2] Nicholas Kaldor,[3] too, found them useful in making a case for his proposal for 'an expenditure tax'. For Fisher, 'income' consists solely of services as received by ultimate consumers, whether from their material or from their human environment which togeth-

1. IRVING FISHER, *The Nature of Capital and Income*, New York; London: Macmillan, 1906. As a matter of fact, Fisher developed this set of ideas much earlier and published them in 'What is capital?', *Economic Journal*, December 1896. The idea dawned on him, according to his son, 'in the summer of 1894 as he drove from Lauterbrunnen toward Zermatt: "It suddenly occurred to me while looking at a watering trough with its in-flow and out-flow, that the basic distinction needed to differentiate capital and income was substantially the same as the distinction between the water in that trough and the flow into or out of it"'. See IRVING N. FISHER, *My Father Irving Fisher*, New York: Comet Press, 1956, p. 123.

2. KENNETH BOULDING, 'Income and Welfare', *The Review of Economic Studies*, 17, 1944-1950, pp. 77-86.

3. NICHOLAS KALDOR, *An Expenditure Tax*, London: Allen and Unwin Ltd., 1955, pp. 54-78.

er might be called 'social wealth' or 'capital'. Social wealth consists not only of producers' real capital such as plant and equipment, but also of what are nowadays called 'common property resources' as well as geological capital and consumers' real capital. In this scheme, 'production' is defined as an addition to this social wealth and 'consumption' as a subtraction from it. Since 'income' is essentially proportional to the stock of social wealth, 'consumption' would have a negative effect on 'income' while 'production' would have a positive one. It is worth recording that Pigou, who took issue with Fisher over this problem, conceded that Fisher's conceptual scheme would be appropriate if one were interested in 'comparative amounts of economic welfare which a community obtains over a long series of years'.[1] It is precisely for this purpose that I propose to make use of Fisherian concepts in place of GNP.

The statistical work involved here is, in the first instance, similar to that of compiling national wealth statistics. But it is not identical with the traditional estimation of national wealth. Although I do not propose to develop a full-scale methodology in this paper, we may take one component of national wealth, namely, the stock of residential buildings, to illustrate the type of considerations we must introduce if we are to quantify social wealth as a welfare-related concept for the purpose making historical comparisons.

The gross stock of residential buildings as a component of national wealth is usually estimated by (1) making tabulations of physical structures in terms of floor space, type of construction (such as wooden, reinforced concrete, etc.), and age, and (2) applying measures of valuation as if all the buldings were new. The net stock can be subsequently obtained by deducting an estimated value of depreciation for each type of structure. Measures of valuation do not usually reflect anything but the cost of construction and, therefore, are extremely limited as an index of welfare. If we are going to approximate the latter, we will probably need to take into account the following items:

1. Arthur C. Pigou, *The Economics of Welfare*, London: Macmillan, 1932, p. 36.

a) basic facilities for residential buildings such as the provision of separate washrooms and kitchens;

b) environmental amenities such as exposure to sunshine, freedom from noise and air pollution, availability of playgrounds for children, etc.;

c) cost of commuting inclusive not only of transport cost but also of time cost involved;

d) shopping conveniences.

Not all these items, of course, are quantifiable; but they are usually reflected in the rent paid or the property price itself or the price of residential land in a *relative* manner at a *given point in time*. Comparison over time of rents or property prices, even when deflated by a specific price index, does not, unfortunately, reveal the real changes over time as regards the various amenities cited above. Thus, a basic difficulty of quantification remains. However, some of the relative rent (or property price) differentials at a given point in time can be utilized to show historical changes in constant value terms. For example, a study by Ridker and Henning[1] – which showed that in the central city area of St. Louis (for the year 1960) a reduction of sulfation level (by 0.25 mg/100 cm 2/day) was correlated with a rise in the residential property value (of $83) – could be used as a basis for making historical comparisons of welfare values of residential buildings. To the extent that relevant amenities themselves are quantifiable and are reflected in real estate prices at a given point in time in a manner permitting a statistically significant inference, we may say that an historical comparison of the type we seek is feasible. As for the cost of commuting, a more direct comparison over time is possible, although the compensating advantage of suburban living is difficult to quantify. On the whole, I believe that we need not despair over compiling a welfare-related index over time of at least some components of social wealth.

If we succeed in making quantitative comparisons of this sort as regards residential building for, let us say, two benchmark years,

1. RONALD G. RIDKER and JOHN A. HENNING, 'The Determinants of Residential Property Values With Special Reference to Air Pollution', *The Review of Economics and Statistics*, May 1967, pp. 246-257.

such as 1925 and 1965, I suspect that the result will show a marked discrepancy between the stock approach suggested here and the flow approach typified by the use of GNP or national income. A rough order of the magnitude of such a discrepancy can be indicated in the case of Japan. Per capita real income in Japan rose by roughly four times between 1925 and 1965 and the proportion of expenditure on housing out of total household expenditure declined from 16.9 percent to 10.6 percent between these years. 'Expenditure on housing' was divided, in both of these years, almost equally between those on 'houses' and those on 'furniture and utensils'. This means that expenditure on 'houses' rose in real terms by 2.5 times between these years. On the other hand, the stock approach estimation shows that per capita floor space, to begin with, increased only by roughly[1] 15 percent over these years and that, according to one authority,[2] the total stock of residential buildings in Japan increased from 9,934 billion yen in 1938 to 10,832 billion yen in 1960; in 1960 prices, that is a 9 percent increase (while the population increased by 32.2 percent over the same period). If we are to supplement these figures with considerations related to the relevant amenities, considerations which are admittedly impressionistic, it appears to me that the net change in the welfare stock value of residential buildings in Japan over the forty years between the middle of the 1920s and the 1960s was, if at all, in a negative direction. Even if we err grossly on the optimistic side, the stock approach gives us at best a 15 percent rise, which is to be compared with the 2.5 times rise in the flow approach.

Although the statistical scaffolding is as yet extremely inadequate, we can at least see that an alternative approach, within the Fisherian conceptual framework, is feasible in our attempt to obtain a measure of the change in economic welfare to replace the flow approach, which relies on GNP or national income figures.

---

1. Statistical studies on this matter are extremely complicated, involving such questions as urban vs rural, the household basis vs the per capita basis, the traditional style structure vs the western style structure, etc. Here it is sufficient to obtain a rough measure of the change.
2. Professor K. OHKAWA. But the figures are still quite preliminary.

CHAPTER SEVEN

The Future of Institutional Economics II:
The Mixed Economy as a Mode of Production

Is there a future for institutional economics? Decidedly there is. Because the problems which are characteristically arising in the modern development of our socio-economic systems – the development which we may designate as that of the mixed economy as a mode of production[1] – require, if to be handled properly, an institutional type of approach.

It may be recalled that I enumerated, in an earlier chapter, the following four common characteristics of institutional economists;

A. the emphasis on the *open-system* character of production and consumption, thus a broader view of the scope of economics;

B. an interest in the *evolutionary* course along which the industrial economies are moving, with emphasis on the dynamic process of *technological change* and circular *cumulative causation*;

C. awareness of a growing need for guidance that can be supplied only through some form of overall social management or *planning*;

D. recognition that economics must become a *normative* science, positively formulating social goals and objectives.

We can see that all these characteristics are quite germane to the analysis of a mixed economy. As Samuelson and Nordhaus wrote: 'Ours is a "mixed economy", in which both private and public institutions exercise economic control: the private system through the invisible direction of the market mechanism, the public institutions through regulatory commands and fiscal incentives'.[2] Clearly, 'regulatory commands' imply some kind of

---

1. I use the term 'mode of production' in the Marxian sense; that is to say, a definable stage of productive relations as conditioned by productive powers.

2. PAUL A. SAMUELSON and WILLIAM D. NORDHAUS, *Economics*, 12th edition, New York: McGraw-Hill, 1985, pp. 41-42.

'social management or planning', which in turn must be formulated only on the basis of definable 'social goals and objectives'. Besides, the development of a mixed economy type of society itself can be seen as an evolutionary process of capitalism and at the same time necessarily calls for a much broader view of the scope of economics than the market-oriented equilibrium analysis. Thus, there is good enough reason to extend the institutionalist approach in defining the nature of the mixed economy as a mode of production.

I myself once (1964) defined the mixed economy as having the following characteristics:[1]

(1) an essentially capitalistic economy; thus the private sector, operating with the motive force of profit, extends over a major portion of the economy;

(2) the role of government is recognized to be positive; and not only is governmental interference with the free play of the market mechanism tolerated (or deemed desirable at times), but the operation of a significant sector of the economy under government control and/or ownership is also considered warranted;

(3) a generally strong welfare orientation and negative attitude toward coercion of any kind;

(4) the state is not identified with the interest of any particular class; and thus counterveiling powers of various interest groups operate.

At the time I formulated my conception of the mixed economy in the above manner, I was mainly interested in the relation between this type of economic organization and the problems of economic development for a country like India. I had taken the view, at the time, that the mixed economy for a developing country had to overcome certain limitations due to the mixture of institutional motive forces. These limitations could be quite real. The reason for this may be spelled out briefly as follows.

The mixed economy, as I defined it then, is essentially a capitalist economy. Growth is a built-in characteristic of capitalism.

1. 'Merits and Demerits of the Mixed Economy in Economic Development: Lessons from India's Experience', in *Studies on Developing Countries: Planning and Economic Development*, Warsaw: Polish Scientific Publishers, 1964.

It performs best, at least in its heyday, when the system is unfettered by extraneous forces. It is not denied that capitalism is capable of raising the welfare of the working class; but it does so only when it does not conflict with the overriding interests of capital. There is no doubt which is the master here. In the antagonistic relation between profits and wages, profits cannot lose and in fact, do not lose in most cases. For, the instant profits lose a battle to wages, the capital concerned disqualifies itself as viable, functioning capital. As a matter of fact, *profits constitute a source of, as well as an index of contribution to, economic growth under capitalism.* Now, what the mixed economy does is to blunt the pioneering function of private capital by encroaching upon its domain either (a) through coming to the aid of 'wages' against 'profits', or (b) through taxing profits heavily, or (c) through narrowing the scope within which private capital can operate.

I believe that the points I made above for developing countries are still quite relevant. However, the problems pertinent to mixed economies of advanced capitalist countries are somewhat different, the reason being that, as in the case of the New Deal policies of the 1930s in the United States, governmental interventions in various aspects of the economy were introduced as necessary curative measures to cope with the near breakdown of the system. These interventions had an ameliorative role to play in an economy which had fully matured as a capitalist system. In fact, a mixed economy strategy was an answer which capitalism had in store − an answer to Marxists who used to say, in the period of the Great Depression, that the contradictions of capitalism were making the transition to socialism inevitable.

Probably, we may justifiably refer to the mixed economy as a *mode of production* sufficiently distinguishable from a classical type of capitalism for the reason that I can at least point to the following significant departures of the present-day mixed economy from our erstwhile image of a capitalist society.

(1) We no longer have untrammeled play of the market mechanism. The extent to which governmental planning and controls are exercised has become fairly broad with all kinds of legislative acts enabling administrative agencies to guide the

103

economy as in the manner of a rudder for a sailboat. Lester Thurow has even suggested that 'we do need the national equivalent of a corporate investment committee to redirect investment flows from our "sunset" industries to our "sunrise" industries'.[1]

(2) Possibly more important than the first point is the changing role of profits in the capitalist system. I said earlier that 'profits constitute a source of, as well as an index of contribution to, economic growth under capitalism'. They constitute, even now, an important source of investment funds which are *sine qua non* for economic growth. What is in doubt now is whether they can still be regarded unequivocally as 'an index of contribution to economic growth'. It is generally agreed that under imperfect competition it pays people to limit the supply of their factors somewhat and that positive profit can be earned as the return on a contrived or artificial scarcity.

There is an even more important point in the age of what Galbraith calls 'the industrial state'. In the classical model of capitalism, most economists would agree, profits were *temporary* excess returns to innovators or entrepreneurs, thus an index of contribution to economic growth. They were temporary because they were, in the due course of time, competed out by rivals and imitators. But of course as one source of innovational profits was disappearing, another was being born; and economic progress continued with profits accruing to successive, successful innovators as a reward. In the latest stage of capitalism, however, giant corporations with oligopolistic power are now capable of perpetuating excess returns to themselves through oligopolistic price maintenance and various other devices such as privatizing particular innovations as well-guarded knowhow. In other words, in such cases profits have become an index of the degree of success in *not* making others share the progress in productivity which in the nature of things should redound to the benefit of all. I may be exaggerating this trend slightly; but I do not think we can deny that there has been an increasing tendency in this direction in the post World War II period.

1. LESTER THUROW, *The Zero-Sum Society*, New York: Basic Books, 1980, p. 95.

(3) Another major category among factor incomes – that is, the wage rate – has also been undergoing qualitative transformation. Let me quote a passage from a document published in 1958 by the AFL-CIO:

Automation in its largest sense means, in effect, the *end* of measurement of work... With automation, you can't measure output of a single man; you now have to measure simply equipment utilization. If that is generalized as a kind of concept... there is no longer, for example, any reason at all to pay a man by the piece or pay him by the hour.[1]

This kind of situation was foreseen more than one hundred years ago by Karl Marx, who wrote:

As large-scale industry advances, the creation of real wealth depends less on the labor time and the quantity of labor expended than on the power of the instrumentalities set in motion during the labor time... The powerful effectiveness of these instrumentalities (in turn) depends on the attained level of science and technological progress; in other words, on the application of this science to production... Human labor then no longer appears as enclosed in the process of production – man rather relates himself to the process of production as supervisor and regulator... He stands outside (*neben*) of the process of production instead of being the principal agent in this process of production.[2]

The insight shown by Marx in this passage is truly remarkable; but actually more prophetic are the sentences which follow the above. He went on to say:

As soon as human labor, in its immediate form, has ceased to be the great source of wealth, labor time will cease, and must of necessity cease to be the measure of wealth, and the exchange value must of necessity cease to be the measure of use value... (Thus) the mode of production which rests on the exchange value collapses.

In this way Marx apparently envisaged the emergence of a new mode of production qualitatively distinguishable from the capitalist mode.

1. AFL-CIO, *Automation and Technological Change*, 1958, p. 8.
2. KARL MARX, *Grundisse der Kritik der Politischen Ökonomie*, p. 592 ff.

But on the other hand, we observe that the present-day advanced capitalist economies, while making progress in productive powers far beyond what Marx could have dreamed, are still able to adjust themselves to the challenging requirements of the 'Scientific-Industrial Revolution'. It is clear enough that at the same time there have arisen certain distinguishing characteristics in our societies which bid us to 'elevate', so the speak, the so-called mixed economy to a unique mode of production on its own.

(4) Clearly related to the above is an unmistkable trend among advanced capitalist countries toward a welfare-state type of society where the precept of 'to each according to his (or her) needs!' is being put into practice. Income redistribution schemes are quite widespread now.

Furthermore, it is increasingly recognized that the quality-of-life question encompasses spheres of activities which cannot easily be translated into market calculations, such, for example, as the conservation of nature, the maintenance of clean air and water, the abatement of noise, etc. To the extent that we attach positive values to these matters, we must somehow make these commensurate with market-determined values and decide on particular actions in particular situations. The decision required is somewhat similar to a decision regarding whether we should expand our kitchen at the sacrifice of our garden within the limited area of our premises.

(5) One final point which cannot be missed at this juncture in the area of our international economic relations is the increasingly important role played by multinational corporations.

One piece of statistics may suffice to impress upon us how important they have become. According to *The World Directory of Multinational Enterprise*, edited by J. M. Stopford, J. H. Dunning, and K. O. Haberich (1980), aggregate sale values of multinational corporations of U. S. origin, numbering 216, amounted to $979 billion in 1978, of which the values produced by their subsidiary companies abroad, amounting to $320 billion, were actually more than twice (222.7%) the total value of U. S. exports in that year. We are coming to an age in which such expressions as exports and imports are becoming less and less meaningful and the entire world has become closely integrated almost to the point of nullifying what was once regarded as the inalienable sovereignty of the state.

Now I have enumerated five points which could be considered as major departures from the classical model of the capitalist mode of production. I believe that they are of sufficient qualitative significance that we may identify them as characterizing a new mode of production for which a term such as 'socio-capitalism' might be applied.

One overriding factor throughout the consideration I have given is the role of technology. Galbraith wrote, as I quoted earlier, that 'the enemy of the market is not ideology but the engineer . . . It is advanced technology and the specialization of men and process that this requires and the resulting commitment of time and capital. These make the market work badly when the need is for greatly enhanced reliability – when planning is essential'.[1]

It is again the dictate of modern technology which almost forces giant corporations to extend the duration of their monopoly and thus to try to perpetuate their excess returns. There has even been a proposal called 'investment patent' by Mr. William Kingston of Trinity College, Dublin, according to which a firm investing in a new product will be given a type of patent that would remain in force and be given public protection until the aggregate profits reached a prescribed multiple of the investment.

The impact of the latest technological progress on wage-labor is patent enough, as has been explained earlier. There is another point however that should be mentioned in this connection; i.e., the broad institutional implication of the robotic revolution in the age of automation. For one thing, robots have the potential of replacing blue-collar workers who belong to unions with white-collar workers (e.g., programmers of robots) who may not typically belong to unions. In other words, technology may turn out to be an enemy of blue-collar unions.

Multinational corporations, too, are coeval with the latest technological progress.

1. JOHN KENNETH GALBRAITH, *The New Industrial State*, pp. 32-33.

107

There are even some people who are beginning to suspect that democracy and technology may not be compatible. Richard Sclove has written in a recent issue of *The Bulletin of the Atomic Scientists*:[1]

> A central dilemma of our time arises from the need to reconcile democratic processes and value with the complexity introduced into human societies by modern technology. How can we keep technocratic *élites* from subverting the traditional political functions of ordinary citizens and their representatives? One answer is so simple – or so threatening – that it is hardly mentioned: Throw the experts out. That, in a polite and restricted sense, is what I propose.

This suggestion, I might say, is in the spirit of the erstwhile Luddite movement; and it will not do. What is required of us is to accommodate the modern technological progress into our evolving institutional setting. This is a kind of task which human societies willy-nilly have always faced in the historic past. It is a challenge which the present-day mixed economies face, and I believe that institutional economics, with the four characteristic strands I mentioned earlier, will have to come to the stage more and more to answer that challenge we face.

I made a point earlier that the mixed economy for a developing country must overcome certain limitations due to the mixture of institutional motive forces. A more general question that can be raised is if such a mixture of institutional motive forces works as a brake for the rapid growth of economies, whether developing or developed. In particular, it has been a focus of debate in the post-oil-shock period whether advanced capitalist countries of the mixed economy type can be vitalized or revitalized to attain something like a 5 percent annual rate of growth in real GNP. I shall now address this question.

First of all, we must make clear what we mean by 'vitalizing or revitalizing the mixed economy'. If we mean simply raising the plateau of the rate of growth of GNP to a level which more or less prevailed in the pre-first-oil-shock period, I am not quite sure I can endorse such *desiderata* without some serious qualifications, as I discussed in the previous chapter.

---

1. RICHARD SCLOVE, *The Bulletin of the Atomic Scientist*, May 1982, p. 44.

But let us concede for the sake of argument that we *are* interested in the GNP rate of growth as a manifestation of the vitality of our economy. On this supposition, I estimate, for the case of Japan, the prospective rate of growth in the coming decade. For this, I take three key variables: (a) capital requirement per unit of output; (b) the macro-rate of saving; and (c) the average working hours. Now, the required capital coefficient, which is estimated to have been around 4.9, has risen to the level of 6.6 in recent years and is likely to rise to about 8.9.[1]

On the other hand, the rate of gross saving, which was as high as 40 percent at the time of the first oil shock, has fallen to 32 percent in recent years and may go down further. Finally, average working hours are definitely on the decline. Taking these statistical estimates together, we are forced to conclude that, at least for Japan, the potential rate of GNP growth is likely to be around 3.6 percent or less. Technical progress will no doubt blossom forth unabated, but it will contribute almost necessarily in the direction of raising the required capital coefficient.

There is one way out, however. That is, to take a view of the world as a more or less integrated society of mankind, in which an extreme degree of income inequality exists between the most affluent and the poorest, with newly industrializing countries in-between. Once we take such a view, policy measures could be suggested toward narrowing the gap between the two polarized ends with the likely effect of raising the aggregate economic level of the world society as a whole on the basis of shifting upward the effective demand of the poorer half (or two-thirds) of mankind. There is no better way of revitalizing the advanced mixed economies than taking such positive steps for narrowing the truly grim gaps which exist today between the polarized extremes.

In conclusion, however, I am inclined to say that it may well be that some of the advanced countries today of the mixed economy type have come pretty close to a stage which J. M. Keynes predicted to be ours in his famous address in Madrid in 1930.[2] He said:

---

1. SHOZABURO FUJINO, *Nihon Keizai Shimbun*, June 22, 1982.
2. JOHN MAYNARD KEYNES, 'Economic Possibilities For Our Grandchildren', in *Essays in Persuasion*, London: RUPERT HART-DAVIS, Ltd., 1952, pp. 358-373.

The day might not be all that far off when everybody would be rich . . . We shall then be able to rid ourselves of many of the pseudo-moral principles which have hag-ridden us for two hundred years, by which we have exalted some of the most distasteful of human qualities into the position of the highest virtues . . . (Then) we shall once more value ends above means and prefer the good to the useful.

Let us hope that our value system will come around to prove Keynes to have been right.

It is paradoxical that an ideal for economists is that they become superfluous in this world as the material conditions of production evolve to a level guaranteeing affluence to practically all the people in advanced mixed economies where J. S. Mill's following dictum may become relevant:

It is scarcely necessary to remark that a stationary condition of capital and production implies no stationary state of human improvement. There would be as much scope as ever for all kinds of mental culture, and moral and social progress; as much room for improving the Art of Living, and much more likelihood of its being improved, when minds ceased to be engrossed by the art of getting on.[1]

Just as the development of the mixed economy as a new mode of production requires, if to be handled properly, an institutional type of approach, so does the coming into the fore of the so-called 'convergence' of socio-economic systems which is the concomitant development with the emergence of mixed economies.

A possibility of the convergence was broached as early as the beginning of the 1930s, if in a somewhat political context, by Maxim Litvinoff, then the Minister of Foreign Affairs of the Soviet Union. An episode touching on this matter was related by President Franklin Roosevelt in his letter (dated November 12, 1942) to one of his closest friends, Thomas W. Lamont, as follows:[2]

In the Autumn of 1933, when I initiated with Stalin the question of renewing diplomatic relations, Litvinoff was sent over and we

1. JOHN STUART MILL, *Principles of Political Economy*, W. J. ASHLEY, ed., London: Longmans Green and Co., 1926, p. 751.
2. ELLIOT ROOSEVELT, ed., *The Roosevelt Letters*, London: George G. Harrap, 1949-1952, vol. 3, p. 444.

had a four or five day drag-down and knock-out fight in regard to a number of things, including the right to have American priests, ministers and rabbis look after the spiritual needs of Americans in Russia.

Finally, after further objections on Litvinoff's part, I threw up my hands and said to him, 'What is the use of all this any way? Your people and my people are as far apart as the poles'.

Litvinoff's answer is worthy of an eventual place in history. He said, 'I hope you will not feel that way, Mr. President, because I do not. In 1920 we were as far apart as you say. At that time you were one hundred percent capitalistic and we were at the other extreme – zero. In these thirteen years we have risen in the scale to, let us say, a position of twenty. You Americans, especially since last March, have gone to a position of eighty. It is my real belief that in the next twenty years we will go to forty and you will come down to sixty. I do not believe the rapprochement will get closer than that. And while it is difficult for nations to confer with and understand each other with a difference between twenty and eighty, it is wholly possible for them to do so if the difference is only between forty and sixty'. Perhaps Litvinoff's thoughts of nine years ago are coming true.

It is doubtful if Litvinoff at that time was able to support his thesis as a Marxist theoretician, but it can be surmised that he saw in Roosevelt's New Deal a trend of the future for capitalistic societies. More than half a century has gone by since the New Deal days and, as has been discussed in the earlier part of this chapter, the mixed economy pattern of society has now firmly been established. Paul Samuelson went as far as to say that 'with some exaggeration, John Kenneth Galbraith and Jan Tinbergen can point to a convergence, all over the globe, to a single modern industrial state – not capitalism, not socialism, but a mixed economy'.[1] Arthur Schlesinger, Jr., an American historian, went further to say that 'the choice between private and public means ... is simply a practical question as to which means can best achieve the desired end' and added that we should 'banish the words "capitalism" and "socialism" from intellectual discourse'.[2]

1. PAUL A. SAMUELSON, *Economics*, 11th edition, p. 817-818. In the 12th edition of this textbook, co-authored by WILLIAM NORDHAUS, the wording is different, but the point made is essentially the same.

2. ARTHUR M. SCHLESINGER Jr. and MORTON WHITE, eds., *Paths of American Thought*, Boston: Houghton Mifflin, 1963, p. 536.

As a matter of fact, Schlesinger's remark summarizes what Tinbergen propounded theoretically as his concept of convergence in 1959 in 'The Theory of Optimum Regime'.[1] He starts out with a premise that 'economic regimes of whatever kind have, to a considerable degree, common tasks and objectives' which, it may be agreed, include (1) seeking to maximize the welfare of the people today and (2) achieving an optimum rate of growth into the future. The two means for attaining these purposes are, as Schlesinger wrote, private (the market) and public (the state plan). Tinbergen goes on to state that the market is inherently better at attaining results where decreasing returns to scale prevail and where there are no substantial external effects of the process; and that the state is the better decision-maker where there are increasing returns to scale likely to lead to monopolies and where substantial social costs or benefits must be taken into account. Thus, if we are to look for optimum methods of obtaining optimum results, that is to say, for an 'optimum regime', we are bound to adopt a mixed system of private and public means. It is almost paradoxical and yet revealing to reflect that Tinbergen, who above all distinguished himself as an econometrician, should be lending his theoretical support to an institutional type of analysis, pioneering as an advocate of convergence of socio-economic systems.

In Galbraith's case, as was discussed in detail in Chapter Five, the overriding influence which technology exercises in modern industrial societies brings about the trend for convergence inexorably, as is succinctly stated in his interview with the magazine *New York Times*: 'the nature of technology – the nature of the large organization that it sustains, and the nature of planning that technology requires – has an importance of its own and this is causing a greater convergence in all industrial societies; ... and in fewer years than we imagine, this will produce a rather indistinguishable melange of planning and market influences'.[2] In the last chapter of *The New Industrial State* where he discussed in the greater detail the converging tendencies of capitalism

1. JAN TINBERGEN, *Selected Papers*, Amsterdam: North Holland, 1959.
2. *New York Times Magazine*, December 18, 1966.

and socialism, both being modern industrial societies, he concluded that 'thus convergence between the two ostensibly different industrial systems occurs at all fundamental points . . . and it will dispose of the notion of inevitable conflict based on irreconcilable difference'. For one thing, 'to recognize that industrial systems are convergent in their development will, one imagines, help toward agreement on the common dangers in the weapons competition, on ending it or shifting it to more benign areas. Perhaps nothing casts more light on the future of the industrial system than this, for it implies, in contrast with the present images, that it could have a future'.[1]

Tinbergen, too, related his 'optimum regime' idea to political rapproachement of the two opposing systems. As Clark Kerr stated: 'he (Tinbergen) visualized "converging ideas rather than diverging" and thought that, to the extent that "there really is a more or less clearly defined optimum regime, actual regimes will have to move toward the optimum"; and he clearly thought there was such an optimum. He feared that any "concentration of political views around the opposite poles" would advance "the process toward self-annihilation". Peace depended on convergence'.[2]

If convergence is the inevitable trend for the future and if convergence is salutary for the peace of the world, we can only be optimistic. A big question remains, which is whether the convergence in economic structure which Tinbergen and Galbraith speak of is conducive to the convergence in political structure. There is no denying the fact that convergence has been much less evident, up to now, in the political and ideological arena; and institutional economists, if they are to be effective, will have to hark back to the broadened approach which Veblen employed in dealing with the politico-economic problems of his day. Then, and only then will institutional economics have a real future.

1. JOHN KENNETH GALBRAITH, *The New Industrial State*, pp. 391-392.
2. CLARK KERR, *The Future of Industrial Societies: Convergence or Continuing Diversity?* Cambridge, Mass.; London: Harvard University Press, 1983, p. 14.

DISCUSSION

For Pietro Manes[1] the argument regarding the *real* and *value* aspects of the production process arises from the fact that both Marxian and Classical economists are searching for a common or unifying factor between them, and this appears to be a mistake. According to Professor Manes, the two aspects cannot be unified. On the one hand, there is *cost* which can actually be reduced to the labor incorporated in the product while, on the other hand, there is *value*, which is not immediately related to cost. Value and cost are two different magnitudes which, at any given time, are absolutely independent of each other. At any given moment, the most costly product may have absolutely no value if no one needs or requests it, and conversely, a free good, such as *natural water*, may assume the greatest economic value in particular circumstances. The two magnitudes become *elastically* linked only in the dynamic process and, inasmuch as value is higher than cost, a productive process will be set in motion which, *after a certain period of time*, will be able to supply enough of the needed product to the market so that value reduces to the level of cost, and sometimes even below it (which requires an adjustment in the opposite direction and a certain period of time). The essence of the production process lies in this interplay between value and cost.[2] The essential reason for so much, and often vain argument concerning the *real* and *value* aspects of the production process, maintains Professor Manes, is that the so-called Marxian theory of value is actually not a theory of value but a convincing and entirely acceptable theory of cost. Value is a totally different concept or, using Marxian terminology, belongs to a different category. Cost, as Marx analyzed it, is the child of labor. Value, as the marginalists correctly analyzed it, is the child of the market. The marginalists' analysis, however, is static, microeconomic analysis which they unfortunately, have not been able to take beyond this stage and which they have then, incorrectly, applied to macroeconomics. Static, microeconomic analysis is valid only under two assumptions.

1. Economic Adviser, R.A.S., Riunione Adriatica di Sicurtà, Milano.

2. For a detailed analysis on the relation between value and price, the reader is referred to Professor Manes' essay on Marxian economics, *Critica del pensiero economico di Marx*, Bari: Edizioni Dedalo, 1982.

The first implict assumption states that *all others things be equal* and the second, that the action of the micro unit have no appreciable effect on the whole. In macroeconomics, such assumptions are no longer valid since nothing in macroeconomics is static, but all things move and change together and the whole in none other than the sum of its micro-units. Thus, the issue could not be settled.

Marx, says Professor Manes, while believing to analyze value, was in effect, analyzing cost. This affected his analysis and explains its unevenness. On the one hand, Marx was able to bring into focus, with admirable sharpness, many shortcomings of the capitalistic system and make some very good long-term predictions. On the other hand, he also made some very faulty and incorrect long-term predictions and was unable to design the means by which to reach his utopistic end. The centralized economy, borne out of Marx's criticism of the capitalistic economy, does not seem to work better than the capitalistic system, let alone perfectly, if the shortcomings of each system are compared. The only true internal contradiction of the capitalistic economy, claims Professor Manes, resides not in the mysterious, or rather, non-existent, Marxian surplus value, but in the circumstance that, in the capitalistic system, both production and consumption are direct functions of employment. Professor Tsuru describes this fact as a *characteristic* of the system and Professor Manes quotes him. 'It is, in fact, one of the most important characteristics of capitalism that what is a cost item constitutes directly a demand for something. Thus, the reduction of wage rates, while it may improve the cost-price maladjustments, results ipso facto in the shrinkage of effective demand'. Professor Manes goes further to say that this is not simply an important characteristic, but it is the fundamental contradiction of the capitalistic system because it frustrates the very goal of the production process, which is to produce enough goods and services to satisfy the wants of the community. The moment this goal is reached, the system becomes liable to be choked by an overabundance of goods which it is unable to distribute under the profit rule. This type of distributional problem does not occur, or at least, should not occur, in centralized economies (except, notes Professor Manes, that these economies do not seem to be able to reach the production goal). Professor Manes then asks, 'What is the solution?' and, in answering his own question, replies that it is certainly not the mixed economy as we know it today, but rather, the search for a system (for which he suggests Professor Tsuru's label of *socio-capitalism* might as well be adopted) which is able to produce according to the capitalistic rules and to distribute according to the socialist rules.

In concluding, Professor Manes adds that he feels he should at least mention another basic aspect of the problem: namely that, in the capitalistic system, some disturbing money and banking distortions exist which absolutely need to be corrected if the system is to be fair.

Reply by Professor Shigeto Tsuru

PROFESSOR PIETRO MANES' comments are very incisive, especially on Chapter One, where I spoke about the distinction as well as the need for integration of the real and value aspects. According to Professor Manes, in the case of Marx, what is called value aspect is actually the cost aspect. Apparently, however, there is a terminological problem which has caused misunderstanding on Professor Manes' part. My use of the terms of the real and value aspects was spelled out quite clearly at the very beginning of Chapter One in the following words: 'The real aspect is physical, transcending specific forms of socio-economic institutions, whereas the value aspect is social in the sense that it reflects historically-specific modes of production'. Professor Manes appears to identify 'the real aspect' with labor cost and 'the value aspect' with market value and says that 'so-called Marxian theory is actually not a theory of value but a convincing and entirely acceptable theory of cost'. In other words, here we seem to be talking about two different things. Instead of using the terms 'the real and the value aspects', I should have probably spoken of 'the physico-technical and the institutionally specific aspects'.

Some of you may remember a famous letter (I believe it was around 1873) in which Marx wrote to Kugelmann: 'Even a six-year-old child knows that if society does not work for one week, we may starve'. That phenomenon is common to all societies, but the *form*, the type of organization which labor takes to feed us, to produce foodstuff, is different according to the system or the mode of production. The type of *form* labor takes is the problem Marx was most interested in. Under capitalism, he thought that 'labor takes the form of value'. This is the point that was developed rather extensively in the first part of *Das Kapital* in criticism of classical economists like Smith and Ricardo. Marx said, referring to Ricardo: 'Ricardo did very good analysis of the quantity of value, but not the form of value'. The form distinguishes one mode of production from another. Thus, I have preferred to refer to the Marxian theory of value, not as a 'Labor Theory of Value', but as a 'Value Theory of Labor'. Some of the participants of these lectures over the past two days may remember that I quoted a long passage from *Grundisse* where Marx said that as automation develops, we may gradually come to a stage where labor time can no longer be a measure of value. In that stage, the exchange economy itself may cease to function, and so the importance of the 'form'. Now the 'form' may be a rather ambiguous term. In the Marxian literature, however, 'form' has a very important significance and the form of value is a thing I should like to emphasize very much.

Professor Manes is of the opinion that 'the only true internal contradiction of the capitalist economy resides not in the mysterious, or rather, non-existent, Marxian surplus value, but in the circumstance that in the capitalist system, both production and consumption are direct functions of employment'. I am not quite sure if I can agree with the first part of this sentence. As I discussed in my lecture, the concept of surplus value for Marx is on the theoretically abstract level of discussion and therefore, it cannot be estimated statistically in the actual world. In this sense, Professor Manes may say that it is 'non-existent'; but there is nothing 'mysterious' about it. As for the second part of the above sentence, I am in full agreement with him, although he seems to think that I did not stress its importance stongly enough as 'the fundamental contradiction of the capitalist system'.

In the early 1930s, when there was a depression all over the world and especially in the United States, there was a heated discussion between those who suggested that too high a wage was a cause of depression so wages should be reduced and those who felt they should not. Some trade unions agreed to the wage decrease. The cost situation, they felt, would then improve and entrepreneurs and companies would be encouraged to invest, thus leading to economic recovery. The other school of thought suggested that the wage rate should not be decreased. If the wage rate were reduced, the purchasing power of workers would be reduced and thus effective demand would decline. Therefore, the market would shrink. It would be better to raise wages or at least resort to public works programs and give higher incomes to the unemployed. Thus, effective demand would increase and the market could expand. This would be the stimulus for recovery. The controversy between the two schools of thought, especially between Pigou and Keynes, was exactly on this point and Marxian economists immediately pointed to the significance of this conflict in policy recommendations on the basis of their own theoretical analysis. Cost is at the same time demand; and that relation, inherently contained in the Marxian *tableau*, was a very important point.

Lastly, Professor Manes spoke of, or referred to, the problem of what I call socio-capitalism, where production takes place according to the capitalistic incentive mechanism and distribution according to the socialistic pattern. Now, in my mind the question is not that simple. Rather, I would say that under socio-capitalism, which I renamed mixed economy, the production aspect makes use of the incentive mechanism of the market and not necessarily 'the capitalistic' incentive mechanism. In fact, the Soviet Union and China are doing so now and, of course, the Eastern European countries long ago suggested making use of the market mechanism in the production process. Oskar Lange, in the 1930s, even recommended this for socialist countries. Distribution, on the other hand, may be described as: 'To each according to his needs'. This is an extreme stand, of course, but we must resort to welfare or social security type measures which the market economies have increasingly done; and therefore, we have defined socio-capitalism in this way. Actually, this is the first time that the formulation of socio-capitalism has been made in this manner; and I thank Professor Manes very much. In very simple terms, we may say that production can be stimulated according to the principles of the market mechanism while distribution makes use of the socialistic principles, combining the two into one organized society. This is the socio-capitalism which, I believe, is developing in many of the capitalistic societies today.

Professor Carlo Secchi[1] remarks that Professor Tsuru, when referring to the mixed economy as a mode of production sufficiently distinguishable from the classical form of capitalism, pointed out a number of significant departures of the present-day mixed economy from the erstwhile image of a capitalist society. Among these, Professor Tsuru mentioned the increasingly significant role played by multinational corporations as an important point within the area of international economic relations.

There is widespread agreement among the specialists in international economics that traditional international investment theory is rather inadequate in helping to fully understand the process of transnationalization of production now under way in the world economy. Professor Secchi notes that various approaches have been proposed, including an attempted eclectic synthesis by Dunning, without much progress, apart from the increased awareness that the decision to internationalize productive activity at the individual firm level is innovative behavior which should be analyzed within the general context of entrepreneurial strategies.

Professor Secchi suggests that the difficulty lies in going from the analysis of individual cases to something which could contribute to the enrichment and improvement of the present theoretical context, in other words, to something which could be general enough in its explanatory power, yet fit closely enough with present-day reality. Researchers in this field agree that international investment is affected by *country-specific*, and *firm-specific* factors, although this is only a first step in the direction of establishing a more satisfactory theory of the transnationalization of production and of the processes of internationalization.

The institutional approach could be very useful in this effort, stresses Professor Secchi, for many of the reasons which Professor Tsuru clearly explained. In fact, it has already been recognized that the first step is to temporarily abandon abstract reasoning and to study reality in detail at the level of the individual firm's experience, in the direction from macro to micro. However, each

---

1. Professor of European Communities, Università Commerciale Luigi Bocconi, Milano.

individual experience is so rich and vastly diverse from the other that, while able to understand what happens in a specific case, it is much more difficult to generalize and build an interpretive model general enough in nature and scope. The growing body of literature on the *new forms of foreign investment* illustrates this quite well.

In conclusion. Professor Secchi affirms that the institutional approach appears quite promising in helping to find a solution to the aforementioned problems and thus, Professor Tsuru's opinions on these matters are of great interest. Of particular interest, reflects Professor Secchi, would be Professor Tsuru's comments on i) the possibility of building a satisfactory and general enough theory, that is to say, returning in the direction from micro to macro; ii) the possible outcome of such a research effort, based, inevitably, on a detailed study of individual firm experiences within their environment; and, finally, iii) suggestions that institutional economics can offer.

Reply by Professor Shigeto Tsuru

I thank PROFESSOR CARLO SECCHI for opening up the possibilities of applying institutional economics to the problems of international economics. The economists I have dealt with in my lectures are institutional economists and, after Veblen, especially modern ones, i.e., Myrdal, Galbraith, and Kapp. You might say that Myrdal was very much concerned with the international aspects of the world economy. He, as you know, was Secretary General of the Economic Commission for Europe of the United Nations and he has written a large number of articles on international aspects, although mostly on the relation between advanced countries and the developing world. Myrdal was very much interested in the question of equality on the international scale and we can find many valuable contributions in his writings on this aspect. But the problems Professor Secchi has advanced are related to the international economic relations *among*, we might say, advanced countries, such as American investments abroad in Europe, Japan's investments abroad in Italy, Europe, and the United States. These investments among the advanced countries are not in the form which used to exist in the past – that is to say, *portfolio investments* or *direct investments* – but very much in the form of multinational corporations.

I cited one statistic to show that, according to the latest statistics compiled by the economists of the United Nations, there are approximately 216 multinational corporations of American origin, and their subsidiaries abroad – let us say that IBM has subsidiaries all over the world – produce and export goods that amount to more than two times the exports originating from the United States, including agricultural products and so on. In other words, multinational corporations of American origin produce and export out of their subsidiaries abroad more than twice US exports. The scale of activities of such investment and production in interrelated form, all over the world, certainly demands the revision of our theory of international trade and investment of, let us say, the 1920s and 1930s.

Does or can institutional economics contribute to the type of situation which currently exists? I think it is a challenging problem, and the suggestions offered by Professor Secchi have opened for me possibilities for future work, and on which I certainly feel responsible to work but have not, thus far, had the time or, let us say, much insight into this aspect of the problem. At this moment, I could add a few comments, but I think I had better refrain from doing so since I have not actually gone into this problem. But, at least I should say that the type of problems which Professor Secchi has suggested are those on which institutional economics, if it can be really useful as a school of thought or as a means of analysis, must work in the future. I do not know if anyone among whom we call institutional economists has contributed very much to this field, but certainly I thank Professor Secchi for opening a new vista for institutional economics.

PROFESSOR LUIGI PASINETTI[1] considers this series of lectures to be a very interesting critical assessment of the deficiencies of traditional economic theory. Professor Tsuru straightforwardly denounces the inability of prevailing theory, which he essentially associates with neoclassical theory, to account for the fundamental phenomena of industrial society, above all, for technical progress. To the points of dissatisfaction, Professor Pasinetti should like to add another aspect which was not developed in the lectures, and which is a conspicuous consequence of technical progress: the reappearance of mass unemployment, on a scale not experienced since the 1930s.

Given the incapacity of prevailing theory to account for such important phenomena, Professor Tsuru suggests a re-evaluation of institutionalism.

Professor Pasinetti remarks that institutionalism has typically been an American stream of thought. In the United States, any time economic theory enters into crisis, institutionalism emerges as an alternative, essentially as a non-theoretical (sometimes even an anti-theoretical) tendency to seriously study the historical evolution of the capitalist institutions. But Professor Tsuru proposes a version of institutionalism which is broader, and which also includes Marxian economic theory. It is here where Professor Pasinetti raises some doubts which he would like to submit to Professor Tsuru.

Professor Tsuru invites us to consider the too many occasions in which facts and theory are in contradiction with each other. In his sixth chapter, Professor Tsuru characterizes the theoretical attitude by a sentence attributed to John Eatwell: 'If the world is not like the model, so much the worse for the world'. That is to say, if there is a contradiction between theory and reality, so much the worse for reality. It appears that Professor Tsuru's response is diametrically opposite: if there is a contradiction between theory and reality, so much the worse for the theory. Professor Pasinetti basically agrees with Professor Tsuru, but would like to insert these problems into a wider frame of reference. First of all, it appears necessary to specify the terms of the discussion

1. Professor of Economic Analysis, Università Cattolica del Sacro Cuore, Milano.

more precisely. What does the statement '. . . so much the worse for the theory' imply? In rejecting the theory, do we also want to dismiss the very process of theorizing? Professor Pasinetti thinks that there is another alternative. He thinks that the alternative to discarding a bad theory is to substitute it with a good theory. Moreover he should like to submit the following problem: If the theory were to suggest an optimal situation and if reality were far from it, how could we consider the alternative of making reality converge toward the optimal position indicated by the theory? From this Professor Pasinetti continues by noting that Professor Tsuru's lectures cannot be taken simply as a choice between the two aforementioned positions (i.e., giving up the process of theorizing or searching for a better theory), but more fruitfully as a different way of understanding the relation between theory and the real world.

Professor Pasinetti is convinced that this different way leaves ample space for the study of the evolution of institutions, especially in relation to technical change, for the study of the inadequate functioning of the market mechanism, for research and specification of relations on the normative, as well as on the positive, plane. In this connection, Professor Pasinetti finds interesting, in Professor Tsuru's proposals, the reappearance of hints concerning value judgments.

The temptation of organizing all these relationships within a new economic approach to industrial reality is emerging from various sources. Professor Pasinetti reports that, some years ago, he himself was under the influence of these temptations when he suggested (in his book, *Structural Change and Economic Growth*, 1981) a distinction between two different fields of investigation in economic analysis. He made a distinction between those fields of investigation in which it is possible to study the relations of an industrial society which are so fundamental that they can be analyzed independently of institutions and those fields of investigation which also consider the introduction of behavioral assumptions concerning individuals, groups, and organizations, within the actual institutions of society.

The first field of investigation belongs to the realm of pure theory. From it there emerges a well-defined area in which economic theory is autonomous. The second field of investigation, on the other hand, is more concrete and, at the same time, more incidental. It concerns the particular institutions of an industrial society and their evolution. It should be noted that, within this framework, the second field of investigation is no longer limited to the contributions of economists only, but is open to the contributions of scholars from all the other social sciences. In particular, with reference to Professor Tsuru's lectures, this second field of investigation is certainly open to the contributions of the scholars of economic history and of history in general.

Professor Pasinetti suggests that the distinction sketched out above should be able to accommodate many of the questions raised in the course of these lectures, and should like to hear what Professor Tsuru thinks about it.

Reply by Professor Shigeto Tsuru

I am grateful to PROFESSOR LUIGI PASINETTI for pointing out some of the weaknesses of my lectures. I quoted from Eatwell, 'if the world does not behave like our model, so much the worse for the world', as if to suggest that economists are arrogant enough to say that, if the world does not conform with the model, the world is to blame. We know that there is a sense of truth in Eatwell's remark. I agree with Professor Pasinetti. There is a good theory and a bad theory. There are good models and bad models. If we can set up a good model and the world does not behave like that model, so much the worse for the world; this is quite true. It is the task of economists, especially of political economists, to develop the type of models toward which the world should work or toward which we, either as political economists or policymakers, should try to direct our societies: and if the world does not conform with this model, so much the worse for the world. I think we should like to be able to say this. And, in order to be able to say this, we should have a good model.

Now, the question is whether mainstream economics (which is best represented by, I should say, Samuelson, and we know that Samuelson not only writes textbooks, but also columns in *Newsweek* and so on where he discusses policy questions all the time) or the models developed by Samuelson and other main-stream economists give us a good guide at the present juncture of the world situation. That is the problem. Therefore, if we can have a good model, let us say, a good system of ideas with implications on policy and so on, I certainly would agree with Eatwell. If the world does not behave like the model, so much the worse for the world. I think I was somewhat imprecise when I spoke by simply quoting Eatwell to imply a type of one-handed or one-sided criticism of model builders. I do take a position of criticizing many of the models which are offered in the economic journals.

Some of you may have read Wassily Leontief's letter to the magazine called *Science* some time ago where he raised a question, referring to a number of articles published in academic journals like the *American Economic Review*: 'How many of the models are actually based on factual analysis, or on facts collected by the author himself?' It is very important that the facts be collected by the author himself. Very often, the facts or statistics which are compiled by other institutions may not be quite the type of basic information which one requires in the analysis one is trying to make. Therefore, looking at the entire academic world, I have an impression that, let us say, the majority of model builders nowadays are not offering us a good theory for the type of problems which we need to solve.

Are there theories, models, in the mainstream of economics which are capable of solving the present economic issues? Well, I was so eager to emphasize this point that I was probably not fair. I mentioned four characteristics of institutional economics: the *open system* characteristic, the *evolutionary* characteristic with technological change playing a very important role, the *planning* needed not only within the firm but also for the society as a whole, and finally, the *normative* type of analysis required. Of course, institutional economics does not monopolize these four characteristics, and some might even say that it is too convenient to give institutional economics these four characteristics. Actually, institutional economists were historically, after Veblen's death, a little bit more limited in the type of analysis which they carried out. Since then, however, this school has expanded in different directions, including Myrdal and Galbraith, and so on. I may have gone too far in including Karl Marx as one of the institutional economists, but according to my definition of the importance of the impact of technology upon the social economic system and vice versa, this relation between productive power and productive relations was addressed most admirably and successfully by Karl Marx. And that is the characteristic of institutional economics as I define it.

Thus, my philosophy in handling institutional economics may be somewhat unique, but I think that, as I have studied economics now for many years, I have become more and more convinced that some development in this direction is needed in our discipline. It does not have to be called institutional economics, if that is unappealing. The current mainstream, or conventional economics, could probably be revised in the needed direction and it could still be called economics. I would prefer to call it political economics. What is currently called political economics could assume the type of characteristics which I have enumerated as institutional economics. In any case, I am most grateful to Professor Pasinetti for pointing out one of the weaknesses of my presentation.

Professor Renata Lenti Targetti[1] finds the *problem* of equality one of the most important and comprehensive issues raised by Professor Tsuru and which could be fruitfully treated by the institutional approach and presents three arguments on this point.

Her first argument considers the distribution of personal income. During recent years, Professor Lenti remarks, economists have increasingly adopted the structural approach in handling the problem of personal income distribution in underdeveloped countries. Professor Tsuru, quoting from Gunnar Myrdal (1972),[2] writes, 'From Mill on, the distinction between the problems of production and those of distribution has been used by economists as a means of escape from the problems of distribution . . . This reflected a bias in economic theory which is still with us, especially in research on underdeveloped countries, implying the view that egalitarian reforms are necessarily costly in terms of economic growth . . . Definitely, the equality issue will rise to supreme importance'.

Professor Lenti observes that, in fact, this issue has become very important in the Seventies, following the failure of aggregate planning. For too many years, the main target has been the rise of per capita income without any attention to the issue of equality. According to many economists, the degree of inequality has even increased in underdeveloped countries. Kuznets pointed out the relationship between the degree of inequality and the stages of development. A structural and institutional approach is therefore needed in order to handle problems of growth in these countries. The traditional approach to personal income distribution, however, does not seem suitable enough to handle this scope.

Secondly, Professor Lenti argues that the traditional approach to personal income distribution is a microeconomic approach. This approach identifies as the main causes of inequality those factors which affect the individual's earning capacity, such as personal endowments inborn or obtained through education in the human capital approach, the age in the life cycle hypothesis,

1. Professor of Economics, Università degli Studi di Pavia.
2. Gunnar Myrdal, 'Response to Introduction', *The American Economic Review*, May 1972, pp. 456-462.

and inherited or earned wealth. Economists have only recently begun to develop income distribution models which take into account the socio-institutional features of the economic systems. According to Lydall, who has pioneered work in this direction, a pyramidal structure of earning reflects the hierarchical structure of occupations resulting from labor organization in the large firms and it is a feature of modern industrialized countries. This feature, as stated by Lydall, can explain the existence of a Paretian tail in the income distribution function in Western economies as well as its absence in the socialist countries. Thurow, following the so-called American institutional approach, goes further in this direction by assuming that the income distribution function is the outcome of a segmented labor market. According to Thurow, the structure and the wide differentials in earnings are a lasting feature since institutional barriers prevent the flow of workers among sectors and professions, which thereby prevent the reduction of earning differentials.

Finally, Professor Lenti remarks that, in all Western economies, personal income distribution, in its final stage, is influenced in various degrees, by the redistributive action of public authorities and depends upon institutional features such as the tax system and the nature and direction of transfer flows toward households. Professor Lenti observes that the reduction in the degree of inequality and changes in the distribution of secondary income in comparison with those resulting from the primary distribution process are *once and for all*. It depends upon the institutional and redistributive mechanisms of public action, without any increasing redistributive trend, at least in the short run. In some countries such as Sweden, where income data are collected according to both the gross and the net income classes (i.e., before and after taxes), the change in the income distribution function resulting from the redistributive action is very clear and impressive.

Reply by Professor Shigeto Tsuru

PROFESSOR RENATA LENTI TARGETTI raised the problem of *distribution* to which institutional economics, or the institutional approach, might contribute. In particular, in the underdeveloped world, distributional questions related to *incentives* have been with us since the development of modern capitalism. In the early days of the development of capitalism, when, you might say, even England was an underdeveloped country and, of course, so was Japan, I do not think there was much discussion, even with Adam Smith, on the question of distribution, at least of the type of discussion which we have today. Ricardo and James Mill were both very much concerned with the question of distribution but their concern with distribution was among rent, profit, and wages – not necessarily the type of distribution problems which we discuss nowadays. Today we discuss distribution problems in terms of the distribution among the working class itself, i.e., high-paid workers, low-paid workers, how to stimulate workers to work harder, how regular wage income should be supplemented by social security payments, and so on. Thus, the problem of distribution is not necessarily a class distribution problem. We used to speak of class distribution, the class of land-owners, the class of capitalists, the class of workers, and that was the nineteenth century distribution problem. However, I think that the problem of distribution has become much more complex and sectorial (within sectors we do have this problem) and related to the tax problem. In most countries, there are income taxes. The issue then is how the income tax and, of course, indirect taxes, should be related to the level of income. There is also the need for government expenditures and so on. Therefore, the distribution problem has become a very complex one in advanced countries, as well as in the developing world. I remember when I was first in India in 1952. India was very poor and is still very poor, I should say very very poor. I was a lecturer at the Delhi School of Economics and I compared my income as a professor of economics in a government university in Japan with the income of a professor at the Delhi School of Economics. I had to use the formal exchange rate at that time since it was the only rate we could use. I was amazed to discover that my professor colleagues at the Delhi School of Economics were earning three times as much as I was. I asked Professor Rao: 'Why is this so? Japan's average income is ten times that of India's'. (I think it is now more than ten times, but in 1952, it was about ten times.) 'I come from a prestigious government university in Tokyo earning a salary of one third of what professors earn at the Delhi School of Economics. Are you not exploiting the Indian public?' And he replied: 'No. We are giving this much service, service which is equivalent to the salary I receive. The signifiance of the task we perform in the Delhi School of Economics as a professor is, if I may say so, actually more than you are contributing in your university. You may be giving a good series of lectures, but', and he was quite frank with me because he was a very good friend of mine, 'what use does the government make of your lectures?' 'Well', I said, 'I am not helping it very much, nor are my lectures helping the Japanese masses, I am afraid.' So he said, 'You see? That is the difference. The significance and contribution we make in India from the profession of professor is quite important. We give guidance to the direction of the Indian economy and so on. And the second reason is that after India became independent in 1949, British citizens were holding very important posts in many places, even the Minister of the Army was a British at that time, and a number of British scholars were teaching in Indian universities. They were drawing salaries which British drew in the colonial period. Indians coming to the universities after the independence certainly should be equal in salary level to the British'.

Now I was very much interested in this type of situation. Many of the developing countries have a type of distributional scale within the same profession, within the same class of people, which is much bigger than in the advanced countries. The margin of such difference is much smaller in advanced countries. Of course, one may earn dividends and interest and so on, or maintain a second job, but regular wages, regular incomes of a certain type of profession have a certain difference, a range of income, which is, in terms of percentage, much smaller in advanced countries than in the early stages of developing countries. I do not know if such a situation has helped countries like India or Ghana. The institutional approach would require this type of problem on the question of distribution.

Of course, there is a common aspect of the distribution problem that the institutional approach shares with mainstream economics: income distribution. The Pareto curve and so on, of course, would help us understand the degree of equality and inequality in a country. It may be noted that I mentioned Myrdal when he became interested in economics after 1932. His main concern was *equality*; in his mind, however, equality not only within advanced countries, but also on the international level; not only in the matter of regular, ordinary, normal income, but also including the issues of social security and welfare payments. There are other supplementary instruments of policy which can make living conditions equal. The institutional approach, I believe, has a broader, open-system view on distribution, not necessarily on the question of money income alone, but also including all other matters connected with the means of payment or the means of acquisition of consumption goods. Therefore, the type of problem Professor Lenti has raised should certainly be encompassed within our view. I am afraid, however, that I have not developed this in my lectures and I would certainly like to take note of Professor Lenti's remarks and further develop my ideas.

PROFESSOR ALBERTO QUADRIO CURZIO[1] thinks that the choice of subject and the way in which it has been developed in the discussion brings new life to economics which is today very often just mathematics. In stressing the importance of economic theory and, in particular, of formal economic theory in his lectures, Professor Tsuru states that institutionalism is a fundamental tool and method for understanding economic systems.

Professor Quadrio Curzio goes on to propose two comments and one question. The first comment refers to present changes in the environment which underscore an economic revolution which is similar in scope but probably more profound than the second agricultural revolution, the mercantile revolution, and the industrial revolution. The so-called technological revolution is in fact an economic revolution and, as every economic revolution, will have enormous impact on society, social relations, and institutions. Consequently, the economist must face a greater challenge. First, he must use his *economic knowledge* in all its dimensions.

There are at least four dimensions in economic science. The first, which is probably the most difficult to make explicit, is constituted by the driving principles on which the economist relies. The second dimension is that of the theories which today is the most worrisome since they are presently dominated by mathematics. A great economist used to say that theories are logical structures which contain the largest amount of information with the least assumptions. Another economist replied that today theories are logical structures with the least information and the most assumptions. Professor Quadrio Curzio believes that this change in the theory should make economists reflect on their discipline. The third dimension in which institutionalism is prominent is historical theoretical analysis, or 'quasi-theory'. That is to say, the analysis of important historical events not through formal tools but quasi-theoretical tools, i.e., stylized facts. Finally, the fourth dimension is politics, which is always present, and interacts continuously with the previous dimensions.

Professor Quadrio Curzio considers these four components to

1. Professor of Economics, Università Cattolica del Sacro Cuore, Milano.

be essential for answering the important problems which arise from a qualitative or historical change.

Based on these premises, Professor Quadrio Curzio asks if it is possible to distinguish among the three models of market economies present today: the United States, Japan, and Europe. The United States is a model of a market economy based on the individualism of the pioneers and on a minimal state. Japan is a market economy which is perhaps even more efficient and which is based on the historical memory of the feudal structure, i.e., a very rigid organizational system with a very precise technique for execution. Finally, Europe might, perhaps, rediscover its roots in the organization of the *medieval town*, that is to say, a system of corporations of professionals with interesting innovative capacity and great internal cohesion. This line should not generate new types of protectionism and reduce social mobility.

Reply by Professor Shigeto Tsuru

In response to PROFESSOR ALBERTO QUADRIO CURZIO's very instructive remarks on certain aspects of my lectures, I would like to first comment on the question of the economic revolution or the technological revolution in connection with the institutional approach. I have taken the view that technological change in the immediate post World War II period has been of a tremendously large scale. We call it the scientific industrial revolution because basic science was, at the heart, almost the nucleus of technological change in the post-war period and was quite different from what it used to be in the nineteenth century. This is probably due to the development of the technologies during the war, especially in the United States, which had various components such as *automation, atomic power, aeronautics, new synthetic materials*, and so on, all of which were used for the purpose of the war. After the end of the war, however, they could be developed and applied for civilian purposes. In any case, science has become the central concern of industrial firms, which implies that basic scientists are employed under management.

Science is a discipline which seeks truth, and is usually considered to be free. It can be acquired by whomever can acquire it. Whatever the scientific discovery it is often reported at a scientific symposium and is shared by colleagues all over the world. Science, by its very nature, cannot be monopolized. The application of science can be monopolized in the form of a *patent*, and so on. But basic science itself is open, is the property of mankind as soon as it is reported. Well, that used to be our common-sense understanding of what science was. But more and more in the post-war period, science has become private property, private property monopolized very often by private firms.

There is a famous case of a certain scientist who was employed by Du Pont in the United States. He was a specialist in the chloride method of producing titanium dioxide, but fundamentally he was a basic scientist. He realized he could not stay with the Du Pont Company and become one of the managers because, being a scientist, his role throughout life was likely to be a scientist. He wanted a slightly higher position, so he applied for a position with one of the Californian firms (American Potash and Chemical Company) which advertised for a scientist of a similar type as he was with the promise of much higher pay and a higher position as well. When applying, he had to sign a document in which he promised not to divulge any of the knowledge or information which he acquired in his previous employment and after he would be hired by the new firm. That was quite common practice in the United States to protect the new firm from being sued by Du Pont. This person, named Dr. Donald Hirsch, signed the document but the Californian firm was sued by Du Pont on the grounds that the new firm should not have hired Dr. Hirsch and should cancel the employment contract because Dr. Hirsch could, by simply moving his eyebrow, or winking, or some such action, suggest when the new scientific process under study by this Californian firm was moving in the right or wrong direction, without saying a word. Therefore, he could not avoid divulging the secrets of Du Pont. When this was reported, the magazine *Fortune* had as a headline, 'Who Owns Your Brain?'

'Who owns your brain?' is the type of question or remark that could not have existed before WWII, but now that science has become the core or the center of modern firms, it is a quite relevant question. I think the institutional approach is the kind of analysis required to discuss this type of problem. The institutional approach would say that in the stage of scientific development – what we call the development of the scientific industrial revolution – science itself becomes a cost item. Science, basic science, was never a cost item. It was free. It was the common property of mankind. Once it is applied and becomes a patent for something, then it is monopolized. But basic science itself was a free good. The mainstream of economics has long maintained this and did not deal with the above mentioned type of problem. However, institutional economics has been quick to realize that changes in technology have brought about this kind of situation, and we have to ask: 'Who owns your brain? Who owns your head?' This requires, I think, the analysis of changes resulting from the technological revolution. The economic revolution, which now refers to the technological revolution, as Professor Quadrio Curzio mentioned, is becoming more and more the type of situation where the institutional approach is needed.

Professor Quadrio Curzio mentioned four dimensions in economic science; namely, 'guiding principles on which the economist relies', 'the theories, which are presently dominated by mathematics', 'the historical analysis', and 'politics'. This formulation reminds me of the statement made by Schumpeter (which I quoted at the beginning of Chapter Three) in which he spoke of three dimensions for the 'scientific economist'. I should like to have heard more specifically from Professor Quadrio Curzio on 'the guiding principles'. But, in any case, I am in full agreement with him when he says that all the four dimensions are 'essential if one wants to answer to the big problems which arise from a qualitative or historical change'. This is in accord, I believe, with what institutional economists consider to be their task.

Lastly, Professor Quadrio Curzio referred to three advanced capitalistic areas (the United States, Japan, and Europe) and their historical backgrounds (the United States based on the individualistic tradition; Japan on the feudal; and Europe with the long tradition of the Medieval Age) which gave society all of what seems to have been relevant in the development of capitalism, yet in different ways. All are called capitalist societies in the broad sense of the word, but all bear the mark of their historical backgrounds. Japan certainly does. As it may be known, Japan has even now the unique characteristic of permanent employment: 'Once hired, never fired'. The loyalty of firm management is especially strong so that once hired, you are trained by the firm, on the spot, and once trained at the expense of the firm, of course, the firm feels that it owns you. Permanent employment has been common. It is slightly breaking down now, but it is, to a great extent, still the case. This is related to our historical background. The position of women in employment again is related to our historical background. Our relation between industry and agriculture is also related to our historical background. I do not know how the situation is in Italy. Italy, in many respects, is similar to Japan. In the case of Japan, many of the workers, or people who work in firms, come from the countryside. They still have their ancestoral homes in the countryside, their relatives still live there, and they return there during long holidays. The busiest rush hours on the Japanese trains and airplanes are the times when people return to and come back from their countryside. This connection, which is still maintained, has all kinds of implications for employment, the conduct of business, and so on. With respect to Japan's feudal background, which was considered to have been liquidated at the time of the 1868 restoration, we can say that drastic changes were made. Yet, in the subsequent development of the economy as a capitalistic society, Japan still retains marks of its tradition. Such traditional marks in our current economic situation can be explained, and, in fact, must be explained, in terms of the institutional situation. We cannot, of course, and should not overemphasize the relation between such historical backgrounds with the current characteristics. I think we can make a very interesting comparative study of the different types of capitalism, such as in the U.S., Japan, and various European countries, and how the historical background affects a certain characteristic of the present situation in the conduct of industries. I am afraid I did not quite answer Professor Quadrio Curzio's questions, but I am grateful for his very interesting points.

Professor Italo Cutolo[1] comments that Professor Tsuru, in his lectures on the renewed interest in institutional economics as found in the works of Allan G. Gruchy, Gunnar Myrdal, J. Kenneth Galbraith, K. William Kapp and the Italian economists, Giovanni Demaria and Giuseppe Palomba, pushes for serious reconsideration of the validity of classical economics. Professor Cutolo believes that the completely new context in which economic activity is developing, subject to continuous technological change, produces modifications in the structure of the system and, consequently, variations in the activity of the system itself.

For example, the application of cybernetics to the productive processes results in the realization of completely automatic structures which determines how the system should evolve. At the same time the new irreversibly modified context induces a change in its structure such that it is the system itself which determines how the activity should develop. Therefore between activity and structure there is, thus, a mutual conditioning.

Professor Cutolo finds that geometry, which is the science of cosmic organization, serves as an excellent guide outlining the behavior of every type of system both in the context of natural as well as social phenomena. He consequently uses geometry to propose some considerations on the principle of unification in economics and therefore, on the affirmation of institutional economics.

The ordinary space in which the accessible natural phenomena display themselves is organized with the simplest geometric logic, that of Euclidean space. This space is characterized by a *metric* which determines uniquely its geometry. *Metrics* assures the *connection* of the space, that is to say, the validity of the principle of the *action in the distance*. In other words, what happens in the *vicinity* of a point is transmitted autonomously to all the points of the space, transforming the potential into the actual. Since this space is *linear*, it is therefore possible from any one point to reach every other point following the straight line which joins the two points.

In addition to the physical (three dimensional) space, one

1. Late Professor of Social Sciences, Istituto Universitario Orientale, Napoli.

could hypothesize mathematically abstract linear space of any dimension. In this sense, the capitalist system working under perfect competition is represented by the principle of *intrinsic connection* and functions according to the principle of self-control and self-regulation or, from cybernetics, the principle of negative feedback, that is, the principle of re-equilibrating action.

The capitalist system, continues Professor Cutolo, could be represented by this model up until the great crisis of 1929-1930, which spread from the United States to the rest of the West. The slow processes of capital accumulation in an established technological horizon, determined, in the long run, equiproportional developments in all the sectors without sudden modifications in the structure of the system. This allowed for a stable economic life because the imbalances created by the development of economic activity were automatically absorbed by the activity itself.

One can consider, however, even non-Euclidean space. The spheric surface, for example, is included in the category of Riemann space, that is, into those spaces for which there is not an elementary connection concept. In these spaces the movement from one point to another can be described only by using the *connection coefficient* together with the *metric*. This allows the building of an analytical instrument known as *Riemann's tensor*.

A system whose structure possesses the characteristics of Riemann space can function adequately only with the continuous interventions of *Riemann's tensor*.

We can describe the capitalist system after the great crisis resulting from the financial crash of the United States in 1929-1930 as a Riemann space. The structure of the system suffered from the substantial distortions, found great difficulty in developing, and it was impossible to settle at a new equilibrium. The interventions of Keynes with his instruments of anticyclical political economy made the system internally connected within its new irreversibly distorted structure.

We can even hypothesize non-linear spaces with variable curvature (for example, an irregular surface) in which, in order to maintain the connection, it is necessary to intervene with punctual corrections of the *metric* which is no longer constant.

This is obtained through the introduction of a particular operator, known as *curvature tensor*, which, together with the *metric*, allows the organization of the geometry of these spaces.

The capitalist system, notes Professor Cutolo, was in this condition when its activity, exceeding the control of the stabilization policies of the Keynesian type, generated further distortions. At that point, the new situation was no longer controllable by stabilization policies organized along Keynesian criteria.

One needs to keep in mind that Keynesian policies are above all interventions effective in the short run and with structural characteristics not comparable with the present ones and with those which have yet to happen.

It is known, in fact, that in the economic universe there are already huge structural distortions whose roots are to be found primarily in the tendency of capitalist production to become international. The activity of multinational enterprises produced structural changes in the international division of labor and in international trade. This, together with the activities of multinational banks, gave rise to catastrophic monetary speculation with violent fluctuations in foreign exchange and consequently, sudden capital movements.

The rapid displacement of industrial production has led to a world economy whose structure differs from the traditional one. The internationalization of production, which is larger than just trade, determined a new type of economic sovereignty. This requires the redefinition of the indicators of economic activity of each country, the national accounts, and the balance of payments equilibrium. With respect to the latter, its costs should be borne by the entire community in a proportional and fair way.

In this new phase, the capitalist system is a space whose logic goes well beyond that of Euclid and Riemann spaces. The distortions generated by technology, in fact, require corrections which should enable the system to stabilize to new equilibria.

To organize a similar space, it is necessary to define *a priori* a law of connection represented mathematically by a particular analytical instrument known as *tensor of curvature measure*. The organizational logic of Weyl space belongs to a similar context.

To give significance to the criteria of unification, which springs from institutional economics and constitutes its guideline, some observations on the logic of movement of an economic system are in order.

We observe that the concept of movement is universal and entails continuous change. According to Aristotle, 'There does not exist movement except for things that move. In fact, that which changes, changes always or according to the substance, or according to the quality, or according to the quantity or according to the place'.

For example, in the study of physical and chemical transformations of an isolated system, the logic of movement is observed through a measure, defined in correspondence to every state of the system. This measure gives an indication of the kind of transformation taking place in the system. The *entropy* (from the Greek *en* and *tropia* which means internal change), the name given to the measure, refers specifically to the natural changes of the phenomenon under observation. The changes imply a dispersion of the energy of the system and render irreversible the passage from one phase to the next. In the limit, they lead, in any case, to the leveling off of all the energy, to which corresponds the maximum value of the entropy since this measure grows with the development of the phenomenon.

The capitalist system, under the hypothesis of a closed market, exhibits growing entropy. In fact, entropy is defined in connection with the capacity of the system to supply to the community a certain volume of goods and services in the presence of a given amount of profits. That measure is expressed by the relationship between the value of national income and the level of profits. The process associated with the development of such a system is irreversible due to the continued reduction in the level of profits and to the resulting tendency to equally distribute income among the social classes.

The entropy of the system grows until it reaches the maximum value which is that corresponding to the level at which development levels off. The energy of the system declines progressively and economic life tends toward the steady state.

In a universe which develops with growing entropy, that is,

with slowing internal changes, the activity proceeds thanks to *delayed* potentials, that is, from potentials emitted from a *source* which is in the past. The operator moves, therefore, in irreversible time and makes decisions based on projections from the past.

There are natural phenomena whose development is characterized by strengthening processes such as those observable in the biological world. In those cases, one can observe the strengthening of a portion of the whole at the expense of the remainder. The processes are characterized by the principle of *finality* with *anticipated* potentials whose source is in the future and, since they constitute the objective of the process, they require the realization of structures which are more ordered and differentiated.

These processes are called *syntropic* from *syntropy* (from the Greek *syn* and *trophia* which means changes in growth) given to a measure introduced by Luigi Fantappie[1] as symmetric to the entropy, for a more complete and organic explanation of natural phenomena in the framework of the quantistic hypothesis.

Fantappie, starting from the observation that some fundamental equations of wave mechanics present two groups of solutions which correspond to the delayed and anticipated potentials, argued that, under some specific conditions, the solutions of the first group could be interpreted as representing waves which diverge from a source and, as such, with a delay with respect to the moment in which they are emitted. The second group of solutions, instead, can be interpreted as waves converging toward a source and, therefore, in advance with respect to the moment in which they are emitted. The first waves originate from the source which is the cause of the phenomenon; for the second, instead, the source represents the end toward which the phenomenon is tending. The entropic and syntropic phenomena present characteristics of opposition, which is, to say, of symmetry; as mentioned previously, while every entropic process is disaggregating, the syntropic processes are instead aggregating since they tend to build structures which are more and more ordered and differentiated.

1. Luigi Fantappie, well-known Italian mathematician from the twentieth century, who invented a *unifying theory of the universe* in which there are syntropic phenomena characterizing life in opposition to entropic phenomena which characterize physics.

In the field of economic activity, the syntropic processes characterize the planned economies. In this system, in fact, the plan (which is in opposition or symmetric to the market of the capitalist system) defines the priorities of the objectives and, therefore, the allocation of the resources in relation to their relevance; the decision process is defined by the constitution of anticipated potentials (achievement of the objectives) which define the stimulus to the activities of the system. The investments are willingly distributed in an unbalanced way among the different productive sectors and the sectors, whose activities are aimed at strengthening the social and economic progress of all the people, are given privileges. In the end, in the context of economic activity, inspired by the optimality principle despite opposite specifications and ends in both the capitalistic and planned systems, the logic of the entropic and syntropic processes with their characteristic of symmetry, appear to be present separately; in fact, things are different, as we shall soon see.

It should be noticed, continues Professor Cutolo, that symmetric logic of development such as the one described in economic activity are found in the entire universe and this should constitute the fundamental principle of the organization of the universe itself.

One should also affirm that each natural process shares both the symmetric logic of transformation: the entropic disaggregative logic and the syntropic aggregative logic, which builds *material structures*. The interaction of these two logics would imply the principle of universal unification.

It was the principle of symmetric transformation guiding Professor Carlo Rubbia, Nobel prize in physics, in his research on the transformation of energy into *material*. This last phenomenon is symmetric to the one of the transformation of *material* into energy (the well-known nuclear energy) and it is unified to this through the famous Einstein equation: 'energy is equal to mass times light speed squared'.

The objective of Rubbia's discoveries, consisting of finding some particles of great importance in order to be able to reproduce the transformation processes, was to unify the properties of the elements which constitute the *material*. Its target was to unify in a single scheme the fundamental interactions of

146

the physical world, that is to say, gravity, magnetic, electric, weak electric, strong electric, in order to reach a unique theory of *material*, and in this way attaining the idea to which Einstein devoted the last years of his life.

Returning to economic activity, one realizes that, in fact, the principle of symmetry of entropic and syntropic processes can be found in both capitalistic and planned economies. In the former, while the entropic processes would imply, in a given technological horizon, a leveling off of the rate of growth, a technological innovation would start new syntropic processes which would allow a quantum jump in the values of the fundamental variables and, therefore, a restart of the development of that system.

In the planned economy, instead, the planning authorities, in initiating a plan (syntropic process), determine a leveling off (entropy) which, with the next plan, will take place with higher rates of return (a better and more satisfactory distribution of goods, both qualitatively and quantitatively, to the population). In both systems, however, economic activity is not stable. This is due to the fact that the microeconomic decisions in the capitalistic world and macroeconomic decisions in the planned economies are determined by unbalanced interactions, and are, therefore, not unifiable in an adequate behavior.

One can argue that, in order to organize a stable economic system, one should first proceed with a correct scientific analysis of the facts based on the two criteria of entropism and syntropism in order to determine the state and structure of the system and the type of interaction between the two symmetric principles. This analysis should be performed using the techniques available today to the economist, i.e., statistics, operations research, econometrics, etc., in the context of economic history.

From the results of this research it will be possible to highlight the characteristics of the universe in which the system works and also the level of interaction between market forces and constraints to planning. In this way it will be possible to characterize the type and dimension of abstract space in which to organize with tensor tools the intervention aimed at stabilizing economic activity.

This is what is meant by institutional economics.

Reply by Professor Shigeto Tsuru

I must admit that I have not been able to grasp the full implications of PROFESSOR CUTOLO's unique approach to the basic question which institutional economists will have to face. His emphasis on the impact of continuous technological change on economic systems has my full accord; but how geometry, albeit being the science of cosmic organization, could serve as an effective guide for the purpose at hand is a subject of inquiry which is intriguing but impresses me as somewhat far-fetched. However, Professor Cutolo's reference to entropic and syntropic processes in the discussion of the contrasting performance of a capitalist system and a planning system is most suggestive and invites us, I am certain, to a closer study of his unique methodological frontier work.

PROFESSOR ALBERTO DI PIERRO[1] comments on the suggestion that institutional economics could and should make wider use of behavioral hypotheses, and, in particular, as it relates to the individual agent. Professor Di Pierro proposes that if one correctly accepts the position that Karl Marx is the intellectual forefather of institutional economics, one should recall that Marx sought to predict the outcome of the workings of the market economy on the basis of objective laws. In his lectures, however, Professor Tsuru quotes William Kapp, who advises us to address the problem of collective choice. Consequently, the approach based on predetermined and almost exogenous laws governing the evolution of the economy tends to be set aside as we move in the direction of an approach based on social choice.

Professor Di Pierro remarks that one must then consider that social choice is not easily conceived if viewed independently from individual choice and behavior and notes that this is certainly not a new issue. Individual behavioral hypotheses emerged with the development of microeconomics, although it must be emphasized that one of the many and great achievements of John Maynard Keynes was his provision of a strong individual behavioral basis to his macroeconomic doctrine.

Returning to the initial statement regarding the need to move away from individual choice and behavior in order to achieve collective decisions and behavior, Professor Di Pierro recalls that the basic argument holds that the behavior and actions of both firms and public agencies can most likely be explained by appealing to the behavior and decisions, or more precisely, to the motivations, of the individual agents who lead or belong to these firms or agencies.

The behavior of collective agents is a subject for scientific inquiry which can be explained and foreseen, to a good extent, by identifying the basic economic objectives or motives of the individual.

Recalling old and well-known concepts, such as, 'it is not for the benevolence of the butcher that we get our meat' of

1. Senior Economist of the Economic Studies and Research Department, ENI, Ente Nazionale Idrocarburi, Roma.

Adam Smith, may not be necessary; however, one may well recall that the analysis of political institutions based on limited economic behavioral hypotheses has been and is being successfully attempted by the School of Public Choice which, it should be noted, has its intellectual roots in the Italian public finance tradition.

Reply by Professor Shigeto Tsuru

PROFESSOR DI PIERRO'S suggestion that institutional economics could and should make wider use of the behavioral hypotheses, and, in particular, as it relates to the individual agent constitutes, I realize, an apt reminder that what Kapp called 'collective choice' cannot be independent of individual choice and behavior. I do welcome this suggestion and I hope that our vista can be broadened to relate the two dimensions of choices theoretically in connection with concrete problems. But, at the same time, we are warned of the fallacy of composition in many instances. More important, institutional economics cannot ignore the point made by Schumpeter, who wrote: 'Mankind is not free to choose. This is not only because the mass of people are not in a position to compare alternatives rationally and always accept what they are being told. There is a much deeper reason for it. Things economic and social move by their own momentum and the ensuing situations compel individuals and groups to behave in certain ways whatever they may wish to do – not indeed by destroying their freedom of choice but by shaping the choosing mentalities and by narrowing the list of possibilities from which to choose'.[1]

1. JOSEPH A. SCHUMPETER, *Capitalism, Socialism, and Democracy*, New York: Harper and Brothers, 1942.

PROFESSOR MARIO MONTI[1] recalls, in listening to Professor Tsuru's lectures, what a Canadian economist is quoted to have said after hearing Professor Tsuru at a symposium many years ago: 'He asks the kind of fundamental questions we have forgotten how to ask'. This can be said also of his present set of lectures and Professor Monti mentions that it is a privilege to have Professor Tsuru present. Professor Monti's discussion includes one observation and two questions.

Professor Monti observes that if one were to recast the contents of Professor Tsuru's lectures in chronological terms, one might entitle them, 'The Past, the Present, and the Future of Institutional Economics'. Listening to Professor Tsuru, one gets the impression that institutional economics has indeed had a very distinguished *past* (from Marx, who has been reinterpreted as an institutionalist, to Veblen, and so on), and may have a bright *future* if Professor Tsuru's forecasts, which will be addressed below, are shared. The *present* state of institutional economics, however, remains unclear. While it is true that highly respected economists of modern institutionalism exist, as cited and referred to by Professor Tsuru (e.g., Gunnar Myrdal, John Kenneth Galbraith, William Kapp), they must indeed be labelled as modern rather than contemporary, not merely in biographical terms, (two of them are still alive and active), but rather, in terms of the influence exerted on the current development of economic analysis and policy. Their influence today, however, cannot be regarded as highly substantial. In fact, it would be rather difficult to name even a few influential economists, aged between forty and fifty, who could be labelled as institutional economists in terms of Professor Tsuru's definition. Professor Monti asks Professor Tsuru if he would comment on whether or not he shares in this observation.

Professor Monti introduces his first question which concerns precisely *what* should be interpreted as institutional economics today. It seems that relatively little development is under way in institutional economics as defined by Professor Tsuru (i.e.,

1. Professor of Monetary Theory and Policy, Università Commerciale Luigi Bocconi, Milano.

an a-theoretical, if not anti-theoretical, brand of economics), while a great deal of work is in progress on the theory of economic, and even social, institutions. Institutions such as trade unions, government bureaucracies, and central banks tend to be treated less and less as purely exogenous factors in economic models. Rather, economic theory is applied increasingly in the attempt to explain the behavior of such institutions through the analysis of the incentives and constraints confronting the decision-makers in those institutions. Professor Monti purports that we have a diverse area of research, ranging from the theory of public choice to the analysis of political business cycles, to name two examples, which lead to normative implications as well.

Currently, a considerable amount of work is under way in which game theory is applied to analyze the interrelated behavior of two or more institutional agents (e.g., the game among fiscal and monetary authorities and trade unions) and even to analyze the behavior of not only the *existing* institutions, but also the *creation*, the *evolution*, and the *function* itself of economic and social institutions.

Thus, Professor Monti's first question is the following: Does Professor Tsuru regard these diverse developments in the theory of economic institutions as a promising, present-day outgrowth of institutionalism because they investigate institutions or does he prefer to dismiss these developments altogether, considering them an outgrowth of the theoretical element of the economics profession which Professor Tsuru regards as being in conflict with its institutional element? Stated differently (and using Myrdal's words, as quoted by Professor Tsuru), does Professor Tsuru believe that it is possible to be an institutional and theoretical economist at the same time?

Professor Monti's second question is more specific. In his lectures, Professor Tsuru develops a highly suggestive framework which leads him to forecast that the role of institutional economics is likely to increase in the future. Professor Tsuru enumerates five points in which institutional economics departs significantly from the classical model of capitalistic production. As these departures take on increasing size and importance, the institutional approach is bound to come more and more to the forefront. Although these five trends have been under way for years, it seems that during the last five to eight years, at least in the U.S. and Europe, as many as four of the five major departures have weakened, if not given way entirely to counter-trends which have moved them back toward their original positions. While it is true that multinational corporations are still growing, the state of the other four trends remains in question. It can hardly be said that there is a growing role for government planning and controls. Similarly, in the last few years, profits have probably been increasingly perceived as an index of contribution to economic growth. With respect to Professor Tsuru's third departure, there seems to be a countertrend here as well since there seems to be an increased inclination to relate wage rates to individual productivity. Fourthly, and finally, one has difficulty saying that the welfare state, in general, is still growing. The question, then, that Professor Monti directs to Professor Tsuru is to ask if this implies that the actual developments in the last few years will play against, rather than in favor, of the fortunes of the institutional approach.

In concluding, Professor Monti thought it would be interesting to hear what Professor Galbraith, whom Professor Tsuru quoted on several occasions during his lectures, would have to say about his fellow institutionalist, and so Professor Monti closes with an *intra-institutional* quotation which accurately illustrates the personality of Professor Tsuru. Professor Galbraith is quoted to have said a few years ago that, 'Like other Americans, I never encounter a Japanese scholar or a Japanese politician without inquiring when he last saw Tsuru. I have yet to encounter one who did not know him; nor have I ever met one who did not speak of Shigeto Tsuru with respect and affection. Perhaps that is because Japanese scholars are politer, better mannered than most others. More likely, it proves that prophets can be with honor in their own country and also the world around'.

Reply by Professor Shigeto Tsuru

PROFESSOR MARIO MONTI asked if we have contemporary institutional economists? Myrdal and Galbraith are quite old now. Kapp is dead. Are there any institutional economists in their forties or fifties who promise to develop the kind of strands which I mentioned, which characterizes institutional ecnomics. I must strain myself to identify some of the economists who could be included in the camp of institutional economists.

But I did mention in my lecture the name of Lester Thurow who advocated the setting up of the 'national equivalent of a corporate investment committee' and who, I believe, is in his forties. I could mention some among Japanese economists; but the western academic world will not be able to recognize their names. In any case, I personally feel confident that institutional economics will have an increasing number of younger economists mobilized into its camp in the coming years.

Professor Monti referred to a great deal of work which is in progress on the theory of economic, and even social, institutions, and asks a question if I consider these developments as a promising, present-day outgrowth of institutionalism. I certainly do, although I distinguish between 'economics of institutions' and 'institutional economics'. The former is largely empirical and yet quite essential for the progress of our economic science. The latter, on the other hand, is theoretical at the same time. Thus I believe that it is possible to be an institutional and theoretical economist at the same time.

However, Professor Monti questions the theoretical framework of institutional economics as I postulated it. In particular, he made critical comments on my suppositions of: 1. a growing role for government planning and controls; 2. the changing significance of the category of profits; and 3. the disassociation of the wage rate from individual productivity. These are, I admit, controversial questions which require more extensive discussions; and I am most grateful to Professor Monti for putting focus on them. But here again, may I say that a longer-range perspective than the matter of several years is needed to pass judgement on the direction of change?

PROFESSOR RICCARDO ROVELLI[1] begins his comments with a reference to the late Lord Robbins, who, in writing about American institutionalists in 1935, expressed himself as follows: 'Not one single *law* deserving of the name, not one quantitative generalization of permanent validity has emerged from their efforts'.[2]

Fifty years later, remarks Professor Rovelli, orthodox economists, while perhaps painfully aware of their own shortcomings in understanding and predicting economic events, would no doubt subscribe to Robbins's statement without hesitation. Professor Rovelli continues by highlighting some of the reasons which underlie and explain the orthodox economists' diffidence to institutional economics. For this purpose, one could look at either the object or the method of analysis chosen by institutional economist. As it would be beyond the scope of this discussion to consider institutional economics within a comprehensive perspective, Professor Rovelli chooses to concentrate on some of the issues which Professor Tsuru directly addresses in his lectures.

Professor Rovelli's first point concerns the *object* of analysis for which Professor Tsuru names one leading theme: the 'impact of technological change on the structure and functioning of the economic system'. On this issue, Professor Tsuru concentrated on six main authors: Marx, Veblen, Myrdal, Galbraith, Kapp, and himself. Professor Rovelli wonders whether these six authors actually share any common point of view on this particular issue. Marx believed that, as a result of the technological impact and through some sort of *dialectic* interchange with the class struggle, the social structure would change and evolve toward *socialism*. Veblen suspected that the engineer would succumb to the market needs of the businessman. Galbraith, conversely, thought that the engineer, or the *technostructure*, would outperform the market. Kapp held that the engineer and the businessman together, would disrupt nature and that some regulation would be required to help restore ecological balance. Myrdal also considered normative issues although his main interest was to achieve

1. Associate Professor of Economics, Università Commerciale Luigi Bocconi, Milano.
2. MARK BLAUG, *The Methodology of Economics*, Cambridge: Cambridge University Press, 1980.

some kind of distributive equality among human beings. Finally, Professor Tsuru analyzes the 'mixed economy as a mode of production' where income is redistributed outside the market system and profits may 'have become an index of the degree of success in not making others share the progress in productivity'.

Indeed, continues Professor Rovelli (and borrowing from Professor Tsuru), 'there is nothing like sectarian homogeneity' which unites these disparate authors. This, in fact, is an understatement. More precisely, it would seem that the most notable issue which links institutionalists together, with respect to the *objective* of their analysis, is their dislike for laissez-faire capitalism: not nearly enough of a basis to categorize them as a *school* of thought.

Turning to the *method* of analysis employed by institutionalist economists, Professor Rovelli argues that i) the methodological suggestion of institutionalist economists is most helpful and ii) orthodox economists systematically outperform institutionalists in the use of this methodology. In his lectures, Professor Tsuru mentions four elements which ally institutional economists *in the same camp*. Professor Rovelli concentrates on two of them, namely, the open-system approach to the analysis of production and consumption and secondly, the dynamic process of circular cumulative causation. Professor Tsuru does not define what he calls the 'open-system approach', but rather gives examples. Therefore, Professor Rovelli attempts a definition, beginning with a description of a closed system. Such a system is one in which the *rules of the game* which agents play are clearly separate from the moves which players make according to those rules. In other words, on the one hand, there is the *law*, which is given, and on the other hand, there is the endogenous *behavior* which is constrained by the rules.

In the open system, the dichotomy breaks down. Sometimes agents play by the rules and other times the rules endogenously change as a result of the players' previous moves. As the rules fall apart, the artificial boundaries between the different branches of knowledge also collapse so that, as technology alters social organization, economics transgresses into sociology, politics into economics, economics into law, and so on. When this occurs, the institutional environment is altered and a cumulative process of change begins, as Professor Tsuru interestingly points out. Professor Rovelli questions if orthodox economists are really unaware of this, and acknowledges that a satisfying answer to this question would require an entire set of Mattioli Lectures.

Nevertheless, Professor Rovelli considers how orthodox economists deal with these *institutionalist* issues, and specifically, the issues of the role of government, income redistribution, and the environment. On the role of government, Professor Tsuru envisages a mixed economy where the government intervenes in the market and is subject to the influence of various interest groups. Professor Rovelli briefly notes that orthodox economists have i) typified the cases of *market failures* where government intervention is appropriate (e.g., externalities and public goods); ii) analyzed the issue of whether government enterprises should adopt a discount rate for valuing their investment projects (i.e., the so-called discount rate) which is different (and typically lower) from the one adopted by private enterprises;[1] iii) analyzed the conflict between liberalism and Pareto optimality;[2] iv) analyzed the paradox of collective choice within voting mechanisms;[3] v) proposed an economic theory of constitutions;[4] vi) analyzed the determinant of the behavior of politicians[5] and the macroeconomic consequences of their choices;[6] vii) analyzed the determinant of bureaucratic behavior;[7] and, finally, viii) analyzed the role of pressure groups in launching government regulation

---

1. Ian M. D. Little, and *James A. Mirrlees, Project Appraisal and Planning for Developing Countries*, London: Heinemann, 1974.

2. Amartya K. Sen, 'The Impossibility of a Paretian Liberal', *Journal of Political Economy*, 78, 1970, pp. 152-157.

3. Kenneth Arrow, *Social Choice and Individual Values*, New York: John Wiley and Sons, 1963.

4. Knut Wicksell, 1896, 'A New Principle of Just Taxation', in Richard A. Musgrave and Alan Peacock, eds., *Classics in the Theory of Public Finance*, New York, London: Macmillan, 1962, pp. 72-118.

5. Anthony Downs, *An Economic Theory of Democracy*, New York: Harper and Row, 1957.

6. Bruno S. Frey, 'Politico-Economic Models and Cycles', *Journal of Public Economics*, 9, 1978, pp. 203-220.

7. Gordon Tullock, *The Politics of Bureaucracy*, Washington, DC: Public Affairs Press, 1965; and William Niskanen, *Bureaucracy and Representative Government*, Chicago: Aldine-Atherton, 1971.

in their favor and the impact of government redistributive policies.[1]

With respect to income redistribution, Professor Rovelli notes that issues and measures of economic inequality have been analyzed by Sen[2] and by Atkinson.[3] Incentive effects of redistribution through the tax system have been analyzed in numerous econometric studies in both the U.S. and the U.K.

Regarding the environment, Professor Rovelli finds intriguing the statement in which Professor Tsuru poses the question of 'whether we should expand our kitchen at the sacrifice of our garden within the limited area of our premises', since it appears that Professor Tsuru is actually paraphrasing L. Robbins's 'relationship between ends and scarce means which have alternative uses'.[4] Professor Rovelli wonders whether Professor Tsuru is becoming neoclassical with this point but offers, in response to his own query, that Professor Tsuru would object to the allusion primarily because there is no market for the garden, which implies that we can disrupt it with zero private and high social costs. Although this observation is true, Professor Rovelli deliberates why this is so and he finds that the answer again lies with the orthodox economists who propose the economic theory of property rights[5] as well as the criteria for economic utilization of natural resources.

While many more examples could be cited, Professor Rovelli mentions a final contribution attributed to Mancur Olson (1965)[6] on the *logic of collective action*, where group action is explained in terms of the incentives individuals in each group have as to whether or not to participate to the proposed action.

Orthodox economists, concludes Professor Rovelli, have a

---

1. GEORGE J. STIGLER, 'Director's Law of Public Income Redistribution', *Journal of Law and Economics*, 13, 1970, pp. 1-10.

2. AMARTYA K. SEN, *An Economic Inequality*, Oxford: Clarendon Press, 1975.

3. ANTHONY ATKINSON, *The Economics of Inequality*, Oxford: Clarendon Press, 1975.

4. LIONEL ROBBINS, *An Essay on the Nature and Significance of Economic Science*, London: Macmillan, 1935.

5. ARMEN ALCHIAN and HAROLD DEMSETZ, 'Production, Information Costs, and Economic Organization', *American Economic Review*, 62, 1972, pp. 777-796.

6. MANCUR OLSON, *The Logic of Collective Action*, Cambridge, Mass.: Harvard University Press, 1965.

tremendous interest in explaining all aspects of social life which have economic implications. They are perfectly capable of practising their science within the open-system approach, in other words, of breaking the boundaries of the narrowly defined economic discipline and of understanding the interaction and mutual causation of the economic, social, and political sphere. Moreover, orthodox economists have a powerful methodology which can be applied to these issue, i.e., methodological individualism. This method, by stressing the importance of the incentives which shape each individual's behavior, is the key to the superiority of orthodox economics. While it is true, observes Professor Rovelli, that orthodox neoclassicalism is not taught to first year students within the 'open-system approach', this merely implies that more, rather than less, time should be devoted to this teaching.

Reply by Professor Shigeto Tsuru

PROFESSOR RICCARDO ROVELLI asked if there is a common characteristic regarding the object as well as methodology of analysis or, to what extent is there a common characteristic among institutional economists. He used the example of the open-system approach. I did not develop what I meant by an open-system approach in detail, so he presumably made his own interpretation, nor did I elaborate on to which extent the institutional economists have things in common in this regard. I should have taken more time in my lecture on William Kapp's discussion of the open system. He has written a book, *Unified Systems of Social Science* in which he has a very detailed discussion of what he considers to be an open system. But a better formulation of 'an open-system approach' might be the one given by Oskar Lange who, speaking in terms of *data* and *variables* in economic theory, stressed the need for paying more attention to *data* in long-run prognostications of economic phenomena. The more *data* are brought into purview of economic analysis, the more 'open' our approach becomes. Here, I may quote again a remark by Myrdal (which I had an occasion to quote in my lecture) to the effect that 'in reality there are no economic, sociological, psychological problems, but just problems and they are all mixed and composite'.

However, Professor Rovelli is quite right in enumerating many of the specific topics of broader character for which 'non-institutional economists' have made seminal contributions. The crucial question here is: whether or not orthodox economists systematically outperformed institutionalists in the use of the latter's methodology. Professor Rovelli answers this question affirmatively. I, on the other hand, am not quite sure. Although I could cite better examples of 'outperforming by orthodox economists', such as Michio Morishima in his analysis of the Marxian reproduction scheme or Jan Tinbergen in his normative orientation, I would rather emphasize the point that a specific contribution on an aspect of the institutional problems does not make one an institutional economist and that a certain philosophical outlook is needed as its qualification.

For this philosophical outlook I counted four components in my lecture as binding institutional economists in the same camp. One of them was the emphasis on the dynamic process of technological change and circular cumulative causation. Professor Rovelli doubts if the six main authors I named (Marx, Veblen, Myrdal, etc.) actually share any common point of view on this particular issue, and suggests, for example, that 'Veblen suspected that the engineer could succumb to the market needs of the businessman'. As for Veblen, I think it is more correct to summarize his basic stand by saying, as I did in my lecture, that technology is the prime mover of socio-economic development and its progress is not only cumulative but also independent of the will or actions of businessmen. In any case, it was a part of my general observation that 'there is nothing like secterian homogeneity' among the economists whom I included in the group of institutional economists.

Professor Rovelli's remark that 'orthodox economists have a tremendous interest in explaining all aspects of social life which have economic implications. They are perfectly capable of practising their science within the open system approach, in other words, of breaking the boundaries of the narrowly defined economic discipline and of understanding the interaction and mutual causation of the economic, social, and political sphere' is quite encouraging. If those whom he calls 'orthodox economists' not

only 'have a tremendous interest' but also are actually producing results in explaining 'the interaction and mutual causation of
the economic, social, and political sphere', I must say that they
are joining the group of institutional economists as I define
them.

PROFESSOR LUIGI LUINI'S[1] contribution outlines the similarities and differences between the theory which originated with Alfred Marshall in England and was fully developed in Pigou's *Economics of Welfare* and the American theory based upon the thinking of Thorstein Veblen, and which was later termed 'institutionalism'.

The Marshallian, or partial equilibria, theory, notes Professor Luini, is an attempt to coordinate and reconcile the theory of utility with the theory of the cost of production: the former is useful for short-term problems and the latter for long-term ones.

Veblen refutes both theories since their basic concepts cannot be applied to reality. The classical theory of the cost of production is not realistic since labor does not consist only of *labor employed* and human activity cannot be confined to the bestowing of productive power (as founded in the basic *instinct of workmanship*). The theory of utility is unrealistic because it is limited to the relation between the subject, i.e., the producer or consumer, and the object, i.e., something useful to be produced or consumed. Therefore, neither theory can explain the connection between basic human instincts and the institutions that limit and modify these instincts.

Marshall's theory, continues Professor Luini, begins with microeconomic issues and, through the method of aggregation where we have a single equilibrium in each individual market, arrives at the macroeconomic equilibrium. Veblen's method differs in that it immediately addresses the relation between social groups and society as a whole. Two main social groups interest him, the businessmens whose principal occupation is to make money, and the *producers*, who work to make products and whose work is strictly connected with technical progress. Despite the difference in methodology, Marshall's representative (and progressive) firm shares a common point with Veblen's *engineering enterprise*. Both authors are deeply attracted to dynamics. Evolution, for Marshall, is possible when increasing returns (or decreasing costs)[2] spread

1. Associate Professor of Economics, Università degli Studi di Siena.
2. The long debate which began with Dr. JOHN CLAPHAM's 'On Empty Economic Boxes', *Economic Journal*, vol. 22, 1922, and continued into the Twenties and Thirties should be recalled. The *net* result was that increasing returns (decreasing costs)

into the economic system, while for Veblen (where notes Professor Luini, we can find the sketch of a cycle theory) a boom occurs when the producers group prevails and a depression occurs when the *business* men group prevails. It is exactly in this argument, maintains Professor Luini, where the weak points of both theories can be found.

Professor Luini claims that Veblen's qualitative analysis of the cycle does not succeed in explaining the forces which act, as in Mitchell's argument, to reach the ceiling and the floor.

The Marshallian analysis, which focuses on the problems of returns (and which has its origins in the old English theory of decreasing returns to land), finds the roots of taxation inside the economic system, specifically, in the existence of rent. Economic development thus occurs when the state, functioning in a positive manner, levies a tax on industries with decreasing returns while subsidizing industries with increasing returns. With this proposition, it is possible to reach Pigou's theory which, based on the divergence between *marginal private net product* and *marginal social net product*, studies externalities as a function of the state, whose role is to maximize *social dividend*.

The interaction between the social and economic system in Veblen's analysis cannot be obtained directly from the divergence of industries' returns but rather, must be sought in the behavior of social groups, where, for example, the leisure class could be a suitable group for taxation.

Thus, it is possible to outline a fundamental difference between *welfare* and *institutional* economics. According to Marshall and Pigou, taxation is necessary and quasi-natural in order to balance the uneven productiveness of the economic system. Instead, according to Veblen, it is possible to have a hypothetical society without a leisure class and with no taxation.

Professor Luini turns his discussion to four outstanding economists, Thomas-Nixon Carver, John Maurice Clark, Wesley C. Mitchell, and John R. Commons, who have been classified by

---

are impossible for any equilibrium theory, but the real world presents many cases of decreasing costs. The new *imperfect* or *monopolistic competition* is the best example of this contradiction between theory and practice.

Allan Gruchy and Professor Tsuru as representative of the second phase of institutionalists. As a starting point, Carver's contribution contains the study of the *old law* of diminishing returns to land but, by abandoning the idea that rent from land bears a different relation to value than does the price of labor or capital, he shows that there is no essential difference between the nature of rent, wages, and interest in the valuation process. Professor Luini proposes that Carver's contribution toward a generalization of the *scarcity theory of cost* is possible if one keeps in mind that there are two problems to solve and he quotes from Carver, '1) What is the best *proportion* in which to combine the various factors?; 2) What is the best *size* for the whole business unit? And the law of diminishing returns has to do with only the former of these questions'.[1]

The young American institutionalists of the Twenties published *The Trend of Economics*,[2] a sort of manifesto, in which John Maurice Clark's contribution, 'The Socializing of Theoretical Economics', appeared. Clark's analysis, as stated in his essay, 'Economics of Overhead Costs', is similar to Marshall's problem of increasing returns where overhead costs arise in conjunction with large fixed capital outlays,[3] but where the contradiction is not between theory and reality (i.e., positive and normative), as it is with the English welfare economists (e.g., Pigou), but between two different points of view for analyzing, with the instruments of the theory, the same fact. Clark stated this as 'an experiment in the simultaneous truth of opposites'. Thus, according to Clark, costs that are *direct, variable, or prime* from the point of view of the employer are overhead costs from society's point of view.[4] The main example of this divergence involves the reduction of expenses through a reduction in the labor force or by the cessation in the purchase of materials, which constitute constant costs for the single entrepreneur, from the producing

1. THOMAS - NIXON CARRER, *The Distribution of Wealth*, New York, London: Macmillan, 1904, p. 65.
2. REXFORD G. TUGWELL, *The Trend of Economics*, New York: A. A. Knopf, 1924.
3. JOHN MAURICE CLARK, *Economic Institutions and Human Welfare*, 1ˢᵗ edition, New York: Knopf, 1957.
4. *Ibid.*

industries. If unemployment is the end result, the productive power is socially wasted while business accounting is positive.

Professor Luini goes on to say that the actual economic system faces variable demand and supply, the cause of which is connected with nature and social habits. The variability of demand is very important for the case in which large fixed outlays play a strategic function. Clark, in studying the problem of *public utility rates*, in particular, of the railway and of electric power companies, discovered that inequalities that arise in consumption (and which are due to nature and social habits) cause an underutilization of fixed capital. This is a case, using Marshall's terminology, of *decreasing returns* in *increasing returns industries* which operate under the condition of partial monopoly. For the case of the railway and electric power companies, Clark suggested that public authorities intervene to coordinate the interests of the firms, whose aim is to maximize profits even if plant capacity is underutilized, with the interests of the consumers and of the industries that utilize services of these firms. According to Clark, this problem is associated with the cyclical effect of fixed capital (i.e., the acceleration principle) on the economy which is the cause of the cycle. Pursuing this line of reasoning, it is easy to understand, states Professor Luini, the normative proposal which supports state intervention subject to an appropriate pricing fare policy during periods of depression.

Professor Luini suggests that the theory of the business cycle can be used as a bridge between the theories of Clark and Mitchell. Mitchell is at the same time the main follower of Veblen's teaching and the most advanced user of statistical tools to quantitatively judge economic behavior and social habits. The central concept of his business cycle theory, and around which the dynamic evolution of society is built, is *present and prospective profits*. Veblen's distinction between *businessmen* and *producers* becomes, according to Mitchell, the distinction between *productivity* and *profitability*; the former can be useful in valuing the variation in the physical volume of product (i.e., net social profit) and the latter in money trade product (i.e., net trade product). However, notes Professor Luini, in the construction of relevant indices of physical production, one encounters serious difficulties when attempting to measure present profits. This difficulty is even more pronounced when determining the relationship between present and future profits due to the impossibility of determining the quantity of capital (either physical or money/credit).

As a result of these limitations, Professor Luini likens the business cycle theory to a box filled with theories originating from completely different basic positions. As a prime example of this, Professor Luini recalls the introduction of Keynesian theory into the old, established theory[1] without discussing I. Fisher's quantity theory of money (and which is strictly connected with the possible separation of the system of quantities from the system of money prices).

In the work of Commons, who 'tried to reconcile the economists from Quesnay to Cassel with lawyers from Locke to Taft', American institutionalists discovered the evolution of the original concept of property from its limited function as a value derived from its use (e.g., power on land) to its value of exchange. An extreme example of this is *goodwill*, which can be considered a generalization of a possibly uneven advantage from the system of exchanges. In this sense, there is a transformation in the work of Commons of the individualistic and utilitarian value of the final units represented by transactions based on a theory of collective action.

Professor Luini concludes by noting that a few years ago Professor Tsuru[2] suggested replacing the GNP method of economic calculation with Fisher's conceptual framework based on the distinction between capital and income, where capital refers to *social wealth* composed of producers' real capital plus *common property resources*. According to J. M. Clark,[3] it is impossible to speak of economic welfare. Consequently, it is very difficult to find a system of social accounting in terms of national wealth. However, if the 'value the market measures need not be the sole

1. ALVIN HARVEY HANSEN, *Fiscal Policies and Business Cycles*, New York: W. W. Norton and Co., 1941.

2. SHIGETO TSURU, 'In Place of GNP', originally presented at the Symposium on Political Economy of Environment, organized by Maison des Sciences de l'Homme, July, 1971.

3. JOHN MAURICE CLARK, *Economic Institution and Human Welfare*, New York: Knopf, 1957.

material of economics, nor price the sole recognized measure', the problem of calculating the social costs of private benefits and the private costs of social benefits becomes the central theme in evaluating every system of the *mixed economy*. In this sense, Professor Luini closes by emphasizing the difference between cost-benefit analysis, whose unsound basis derives from welfare economics and the Fisherian method revised by Professor Tsuru.

Reply by Professor Shigeto Tsuru

PROFESSOR LUIGI LUINI referred to cost-benefit analysis and I believe he in effect asked the question: 'Do institutional economists have any unique way of making use of cost-benefit analysis?' I think they do. Institutional economists, as I consider them, have been discussing what we call '*social* cost-benefit analysis', not only costs and benefits which are quantifiable in the standard way, but social costs and social benefits which can certainly be interpreted in terms of the open system. Some social costs and social benefits are not quantifiable. When some of the costs and benefits are not quantifiable, how can we have cost-benefit analysis? This is a problem which has been plaguing us quite a bit, for example, in connection with the lastest discussion we were having on the Japanese National Railroad. Just like in Italy, Japan is having a crisis in its national railroad: a tremendous amount of deficit has been accumulated. The cost-benefit analysis that had been made on the national railroad has been rather unfavorable; thus, many of us, political economists you might say, came up with the suggestion of making a *social* cost-benefit analysis. For example, travelling along the railroad gives you a much greater appreciation of the natural beauties of Japan. There are much less accidents and the cost of transportation is much less using the railroad than using automobiles, and so on. All kinds of things can be included in the cost-benefit analysis, some of which are not quantifiable. As for costs, we probably have to include the noise caused by rapid trains, a social cost which is not easily quantifiable. Therefore, when we began discussing social cost-benefit analysis, we needed to introduce orientations of institutional economists.

Professor Luini's discussions of Veblen in comparison with Marshall and Pigou extending to the observations on Carver, John Maurice Clark, Mitchell and Commons are highly suggestive; and I am certain that they call for a fuller treatment than I can give on this occasion. I excuse myself from doing this mainly on the ground that the topic is somewhat tangential to the main theme of my lectures.

PROFESSOR ORLANDO D'ALAURO[1] makes a brief remark on Professor Tsuru's thoughts regarding Professor Secchi's comments. Professor D'Alauro believes that in a mixed economy where, as Professor Tsuru has emphasized, multinational corporations rule international trade, the general principles of the theory cannot be neglected. The fundamental Hecksher-Olin theory cannot be disregarded since the multinational corporations also take into account the prices of the factors of production for every decision concerning firm location, or relocation, and then fix the optimal combination of the factors.

Professor D'Alauro then asks if the decreasing signifiance of the concept of exports and imports resulting from increased real integration of the world economy will bring about a fundamental change in the concept of disequilibrium (and especially, the concept of deficit) in the balance of trade and thereby diminish the importance of monetary policy for re-establishing equilibrium in international trade, and especially in defending the international value of moneys in various countries.

Reply by Professor Shigeto Tsuru

Finally, PROFESSOR ORLANDO D'ALAURO questioned the relation between international economics and international trade theory. Multinational corporations have certainly been on the increase. However, international trade theory, of the mainstream economic type, can be applied to most of the phenomena of international trade problems. Transfer pricing, for example, can certainly be analyzed in terms of traditional economics. The present-day economic friction between Japan and Western Europe, Japan and the United States, can also be discussed in terms of traditional international trade theory. However, there are various areas in the international scene where mainstream economics is having difficulty predicting what is going to happen. The best example is the *flexible exchange rate*. The flexible exchange rate was considered to be adequate in coping with the problems of current international trade relations or exchange

---

1. Professor of Economic and Financial Policy, Università degli Studi di Genova.

relation problems. The hope was that isolating the impact of monetary conditions of country A upon country B would prevent the spillover of inflation from country A to country B. It turned out to be otherwise. The United States, for example, maintains very high interest rates along with its foreign trade deficit. Japan, attracted by the U.S. high interest rates, exports its capital to the United States, selling yen for dollars with the result of cheapening yen. Thus, the U.S. monetary situation is to export to Japan an inflationary impact through this type of mechanism. The mechanism, which is rather complicated but which is going on nonetheless, is becoming more and more distinct from the type which traditional international finance or trade theories predicted it would be. Therefore, although institutional economics is still not quite equal in handling the question of international trade theory in a systematic way, I still feel that, in many respects, mainstream economics requires revisions which border on the type of things which institutional economics suggests.

BIOGRAPHY
of Shigeto Tsuru

1. Biographical Note

SHIGETO TSURU was born on March 6, 1912 in Tokyo to a traditional Japanese family. His father, an engineer, impressed by the fact that Japan lacked competent diplomats when, after the Russo-Japanese War ended, Japan won but was said to have 'lost' in the post-war diplomacy, encouraged Tsuru to pursue a diplomatic career. In 1929, Tsuru began his higher education along an *elite* course of study toward the Law Department of Tokyo Imperial University.

The end of his first year of higher school coincided with Japanese military intervention in China and many sensitive Japanese youth interpreted these events as evidence vindicating the Marxist-Leninist thesis of capitalism's crisis and imperialism's aggression. In this intellectual climate, Tsuru also became active in the then fashionable student movement opposing military training in schools and began organizing study groups on Marxism. A wave of suppression swept over many of the campuses as a consequence of such activities in 1930 and Tsuru was arrested for detention and expelled from the school. He was released after three months due to his minor-age but was prohibited from continuing his education in Japan.

Prompted by his father, Tsuru decided to go abroad for study. In those days, Germany was considered the academic *mecca* in the minds of most Japanese, whereas the general impression was that only the playboy type of *elitist* youth would go to the United States. Thus, Germany was Tsuru's preference, in addition to the fact that German was his first foreign language. However, given that the Marxist-oriented Social Democratic party was quite strong then in Germany, Tsuru's father agreed to finance his studies only under the condition that he pursue them in the United States. Aware that a large number of immigrants from Germany who had escaped from the persecution of Bismarck resided in northern Wisconsin, he chose to study at Lawrence College in Appleton, Wisconsin and on September 18, 1931, he began his matriculation, with a clandestine intention of eventually transferring to Germany.

With the *Reichstag* fire of February 1933 and the rise of Hitler

173

to power in Germany, it became clear to Tsuru that the possiblity of the free pursuit of science in Germany was no longer an option and so he had to choose between remaining at Lawrence or moving on to a big-time institute such as Harvard. At Lawrence, Tsuru was trying his hand at experimental psychology and his first publication in an academic journal was on the subject of 'The Meaning of Meaning'. Some of his other work in that field focused on 'Some Neurological Consideration of the Vitalism vs. Mechanism Controversy'.

Tsuru was also fortunate to have had at Lawrence as his mentor, Gordon Clapp, who was then Dean of Students and who later became Board Director of the Tennessee Valley Authority. Clapp advised Tsuru to transfer to Harvard College for his junior year and in September 1933, having given up the idea of going to Germany, Tsuru moved to Cambridge, Mass. At Harvard, Tsuru was not sure of what to major in and registered in the Division of History, Government and Economics, meanwhile taking advantage of the access to the great minds which shined on the campus, notably, Alfred North Whitehead in philosophy and Crane Brinton in history. At the same time, he continued his experiments which he had conducted in relation to his 1932 article on 'The Meaning of Meaning' with unexpectedly strong encouragement from Gordon Allport, professor of social psychology.

Economics still interested Tsuru in spite of his varied interests and he decided to write his Honor's Thesis on 'An Aspect of Marx's Methodology in Economics: "the Fetishism of Commodities"' for his bachelor's degree – a subject matter which almost half a century later still occupies a *niche* in the corner of his mind. Most memorable among the unsystematic courses in economics that Tsuru followed at Harvard was a half-year course on 'Value and Distribution' given by Frank W. Taussig, famous for his Socratic method and who was in his last year of teaching at Harvard. It was probably Taussig more than anyone else who inspired Tsuru to go on to graduate school in economics.

Tsuru moved on to graduate school at Harvard in the fall of 1935. The graduate student body at Harvard during the years 1935 to 1938 was of extremely high calibre. His graduate class included some of the most brilliant aspirants in the profession such as Paul Samuelson, Robert Triffin, and Robert Bryce who, along with those who had come there earlier, such as John K. Galbraith, Richard Musgrave, Abe Bergson, Paul Sweezy, and Wolfgang Stopler, created an unusually stimulating atmosphere of mutual edification. Soon to follow this group were, among others, Evsey Domar, Sidney Alexander, James Tobin, Joe Bain, and Robert Solow.

At the same time, the economics faculty at Harvard saw the arrival of economists such as Schumpeter, Haberler, Leontief, and Alvin Hansen who were in their prime and Tsuru and his student colleagues benefitted greatly from their instructions. The presence of this group of faculty attracted visiting scholars from abroad among which included Oscar Lange, Abba Lerner, Paul Baran, Eric Roll, N. Kaldor, F. Machlup, N. Gerogescu-Roegen, Oscar Morgenstern, and Jacob Marschak, with whom there was occasion almost daily for heated discussions on the state of economic science among both students and faculty. In addition, Keynes' *General Theory*, published during Tsuru's years as a graduate student, was a great influence on him as he and most of his colleagues gathered together to test their understanding of the new vista opened by that genius.

In response to political developments throughout the world in the years 1936 and 1937, Tsuru became involved with a group of young Marxist scholars in Cambridge, Massachusetts which began publishing *Science and Society – A Marxian Quarterly*, an academic journal with a Marxian orientation and which had its first number published in October 1936.

Japan's invasion of China, which had begun with the Manchurian Incident of September 1931 and which continued to escalate until its peak in 1937, occupied a substantial portion of Tsuru's time. He worked closely with some of the people associated with the Institute of Pacific Relations in New York in the journalistic campaign and often wrote in a magazine entitled *Amerasia*. He also drafted for the Chinese Council of Economic Research a lengthy pamphlet, *Japan's Economy Under Strain*, trying to show deteriorating economic conditions in Japan.

While working toward the completion of his doctoral dissertation, Tsuru engaged in debate with Maurice Dobb on Marx's theory of value pointing out the importance of the *qualitative* aspect of the value theory in Marx while criticizing Dobb for having concentrated too much on the *quantitative* aspect and for posing the question in terms of a 'general concept of value' and its *desiderata*. Tsuru's article appeared over the *nom de plume* of Alfred Lowe in the pre-war English review *The Modern Quarterly* in July 1938 under the title of 'Mr. Dobb and Marx's Theory of Value'.

Tsuru also debated with Kei Shibata on the falling tendency of the rate of profit which was first conducted in Japanese in 1937 on the pages of *Keizai Ronso* – the journal published by the economics department of Kyoto University. Tsuru also wrote a less technical version of the debate in English in the same year, although it was first published in 1951 in *Keizai Kenkyu* – the journal of the Institute of Economic Research, Hitotsubashi University.

Tsuru married Masako Wasa in Tokyo in June 1939 and she returned with him to Cambridge to spend the final year before completion of his dissertation. In May 1940, Tsuru completed his doctoral dissertation, 'Business Cycles Theorie and Their Application to Japan'. Although it was never published, a summary of its empirical parts was written in article form and published in *The Review of Economics and Statistics* in November 1941.

After receiving his degree, Tsuru decided to remain in the United States and seek a position in one of the American universities rather than return to Japan. While waiting for a possible opening, the economics department of Harvard supported him with assistant positions for a number of professors, including Haberler, Leontief, Seymour Harris, and Paul Sweezy. His postdoctoral research was inevitably somewhat wide-ranging. For Haberler, Tsuru worked on quantitative trade-control; for Leontief, on the treatment of the government sector in his input-output analysis; for Harris, he assisted with his course on 'Economics of War'; and for Sweezy, they worked together on his course on 'Marxian Economics'. During this interlude, Tsuru published two articles: one 'On Reproduction Schemes' which appeared as an appendix to Paul Sweezy's *The Theory of Capitalist Development*,

1942, related the steady and expanded reproduction schemes of Marx to Quesnay's *tableau economique* and to the Keynesian aggregates; and another 'Business Cycles and Capitalism – Schumpeter vs Marx' which was published much later in 1956 in Tsuru's *Essays on Marxian Economics*.

When, on December 7, 1941, Japan started war with the United States, Tsuru found himself classified as an 'enemy alien' subject to various restrictions on his conduct, including the temporary freezing of his bank account. Nothing changed, however, regarding his relations with Harvard University. He continued to draw a salary from the university for assisting Harris in his course on 'Economics of War' and for various other research jobs.

Although the initial phase of the Pacific War was somewhat one-sided for Japan, Tsuru was convinced that eventually Japan would be defeated and he began harboring the idea, as early as the spring of 1942, of returning home so that he could be of some service during the period of post-war reconstruction. His first chance of repatriation came in early June 1942 on an exchange basis mainly for diplomatic corps and people classified as 'international merchants' (both of whom had been kept in informal confinement at luxury hotels after the outbreak of the war). Tsuru and his wife were allocated berths only on sufferance on the exchange ship. Because no paper material was allowed on board and each person was limited to 32 cubic feet for Tsuru's status, he had to leave behind his entire collection of books, documents and writings (the second time he lost it, the first being when he was arrested in 1930) and his wife had to surrender all her music scores as well as her cherished amulets.

On Tsuru's arrival back to Japan toward the end of August 1942, he had no stable job awaiting him. After 'loafing' for almost one year, Professor Yasaka Takagi reintroduced him to the academic world by suggesting that Tsuru give a series of lectures at Tokyo Imperial University on the subject of 'Politics and Economic Policies in the United States'. The lectures were subsequently published in book form and attracted some attention as an 'unusually objective book on our enemy country'. Soon after, Tsuru was employed on a temporary basis by the Research Institute which later came to be known as the Institute of Economic Research, Hitotsubashi University. It was at that time that he wrote an article on 'Reflections on the National Income Concept', the subject of which remained his major concern in the subsequent years.

In June of 1944, Tsuru was called to duty as a private in one of the infantry regiments in Kyushu, but, to his surprise, some people in the Foreign Office who apparently knew of Tsuru worked for an exceptional discharge for him from military duty in order that his professional qualifications could be better utilized in the foreign service. He was thus discharged and returned to Tokyo, where he was soon after appointed as a diplomatic officer. It was in this capacity that Tsuru went to the Soviet Union in the spring of 1945, personally escaping the severest air raids on Tokyo but finding his library burnt to ashes on his return.

Three years after the end of the war, Tsuru returned to his professional career as an economist. But during those three years, many things happened to him.

When General Douglas MacArthur landed in Japan as the Supreme Commander of Allied Powers (SCAP), he found the Japanese economy in shambles. The occupation was to continue until the Peace Treaty had been signed and came into force, which was several years away; and until then it was the responsibility of the SCAP to maintain law and order in Japan, for which the minimum requirements were reasonable stability in the economic sphere. The Economic and Scientific Section (ESS) was in charge of this, but it was headed by a military man, General Marquet of the artillary division. Therefore, the SCAP requested the Japanese government send in a 'competent economist with good facility in the English language'. Tsuru was chosen from within the Foreign Office and from April 1946, he became economic advisor to the ESS.

The first post-war general elections took place one year later and the Socialist Party obtained the plurality; and as a consequence, a coalition cabinet was formed with Mr. Tetsu Katayama, a socialist, as the Prime Minister. At this juncture, the SCAP ordered a radical reform in the organization of the Economic Stabilization Board (ESB) in the Japanese government, creating four vice-ministers and transferring some of the major administrative powers from other ministries. General Marquet of the ESS suggested to Tsuru that he go into this newly strenthened ESB as one of the vice-ministers. Tsuru did so and remained in that post until the Katayama Cabinet fell in February 1948. Of Tsuru's many accomplishments during that hectic period of Japan's post-war reconstruction as part of the ESS and then the ESB, one of his most notable was the drafting of the first Economic White Paper for the ESB in July 1947, which was accomplished under his leadership and which initiated the tradition of annual publications in subsequent years.

After his resignation from the government post, Tsuru received a number of academic offers but decided to return, in September 1948, to Hitotsubashi University, which had been reorganized in the post-war period into a multi-faculty social science university. This time, Tsuru's association with Hitotsubashi lasted for twenty-seven years until March 1975 when he retired from the presidency of that university.

Upon returning to an academic post, Tsuru began to reinitiate contact with previous teachers and colleagues at Harvard, reporting on his professional rambling till then and requesting them to send the books and journals in the economic field which they could spare. From these responses, Tsuru and Hitotsubashi were brought up to date on the post-war publications in the United States. At the Institute of Economic Research of Hitotsubashi, Tsuru's fields of research shifted back and forth rather widely, but with a fair degree of concentration on the following topics: (i) statistical and theoretical studies on *national income* and related concepts; (ii) theoretical and empirical analyses in the field of *economic development*; (iii) theoretical and historical studies of *capitalist societies*, especially of Japan; (iv) empirical analyses of the *contemporary Japanese economy*; (v) political economy of *environmental pollution*; and finally, (vi) the present-day significance of *Marxian economics*. (Most of Tsuru's articles in these fields are included in the 13 volumes of his *Collected Works*, of which volumes 1 to 12 are in Japanese.)

Even while holding a chair in Hitotsubashi University, Tsuru's

179

peripatetic propensity persisted both physically and intellectually. He went abroad quite often as visiting professor to the Delhi School of Economics (1952-1953), Harvard (1956-1957), the University of British Columbia (1958-1959), Yale (1960), the Johns Hopkins University (1960-1961), Rochester (1961), and Harvard again (1970). He served twice as economic officer in ECAFE in Bangkok (1954 and 1955). In 1964 he made a memorable trip as a Dyason Lecturer to Australia. A SEANZA[1] Central Banking Course lectureship took Tsuru to Pakistan (1964) and New Zealand (1965). He also took numerous brief visits to Europe and elsewhere in his capacities as vice-president of the International Social Science Council (ISSC) and as president of the International Economic Association, in addition to frequent attendances at symposia on specific subjects. One such symposium organized by Tsuru in Tokyo in 1970 for the ISSC on 'Economics of Environmental Disruption' was the occasion when the famed 'Tokyo Resolution' was adopted and which urged 'the adoption in law of the principle that every person is entitled by right to the environment free of elements which infringe human health and well-being and the nature's endowment, including its beauty, which shall be the heritage of the present to the future generations'.

In addition to his professional activities as an economist, Tsuru participated actively in the journalistic campaign for an 'all-inclusive peace treaty' organized in 1948 by 'The Forum on Peace Problems'. The campaign was interpreted by the U.S. authorities as 'anti-American' and Tsuru's association with this forum became one of the grounds, he suspects, for the later molestation he suffered from the U.S. Congressional Committee in the MacArthy period and beyond.

After leaving Hitotsubashi University, Tsuru served, from 1975 to 1985, as editorial advisor to *Asahi Shimbun*, the well-known and widely circulated Japanese newspaper. And from 1986 to 1990, he held a professorship in the Faculty of International Studies at Meiji Gakuin University.

Tsuru wrote for publications on sundry subjects other than

1. South-East Asia, New Zealand and Australia

economics, though only a few in English. One such article was 'Japanese Images of America' contained as the last chapter in *Paths of American Thought* (1963) edited by Arthur M. Schlesinger, Jr. and Morton White, to which a reviewer commented in *The Economist* (May 2, 1964): 'The editors of this fascinating volume wind up their domestic mind-crawling with three sets of home thoughts from abroad: American and Europe, each viewing each – the two-way mirror; and, most original and questioning of all, a Japanese scholar's depiction of the images of America by his countrymen. It makes a fitting climax to a continously lively and quickening collection'.

Tsuru summarizes his current thoughts, though rooted in the past, on how Japan should, and actually can, guide its national policies in the context of the present international situation in an article entitled 'Whither Japan? – A Positive Program of Nation-Building in the Age of Uncertainty' (available in English in *Japan Quarterly*, Oct.-Dec. 1980). Two concrete themes run throughout the article: one to the effect that 'we are entering a new age of "restoration of man" in which man, the sun and green shall prevail and not the large cities or industries'; the other that the Japanese Peace Constitution,[1] unique in the world, should be made the mainstay of the nation's foreign policy.

Shigeto Tsuru is presently Chairman of Village Shonan Incorporated in Yokohama, a center for international scientific and cultural exchange planned for the initiation of its activities in 1993.

---

1. It contains an article which reads: 'Aspiring sincerely to an international peace based on justice and order, the Japanese people forever renounce war as a sovereign right of the nation and the threat or use of force as a means of settling international disputes.

In order to accomplish the aim of the preceeding paragraph, land, sea, and air forces as well as other war potential will never be maintained. The right of belligerency of the State will not be recognized'.

2. Bibliography

1. *Books and Articles (in English and French)*

'On Reproduction Schemes', in *The Theory of Capitalist Development*, edited by Paul M. Sweezy, New York: Oxford University Press, 1942, appendix.

'Toward Economic Stability in Japan', in *Pacific Affairs*, vol. 22, n. 4, 1946.

'America's Economic Dilemma', in *Contemporary Japan*, 1947.

'Long-Term Changes in the National Product of Japan Since 1875', co-authored by K. Ohkawa, C. Takahashi, and I. Yamada, presented at the Conference of the International Association for Research in Income and Wealth, 1951.

'Marx's Theory of the Falling Tendency of the Rate of Profit', *The Economic Review*, July 1951, pp. 190-199.

'Business Cycle and Capitalism: Schumpeter versus Marx', in *The Annals of the Hitotsubashi Academy*, vol. 2, n. 2, 1952.

'Marx's Tableau Economique and "Underconsumption" Theory', *The Indian Economic Review*, February 1953, pp. 1-13.

'Le yen japonais', in *Revue de Science et de Legislation Financières*, 1953.

'Keynes versus Marx: The Methodology of Aggregates', in *Post-Keynesian Economics*, edited by Kenneth K. Kurihara, Rutgers University Press, 1954.

'On the Soviet Concept of National Income', in *The Annals of the Hitotsubashi Academy*, vol. 5, n. 1, October 1954.

'Business Cycles in Post-War Japan', in *The Business Cycle in the Post-War World*, edited by E. Lundberg, London: Macmillan, 1955.

'A New Japan? Political, Economic, and Social Aspects of Postwar Japan', in *The Atlantic Monthly*, January 1955.

Essays on Marxian Economics, Tokyo: The Science Council of Japan, Economic Series N. 8, Kinokuniya Co., Ltd., 1956.

'Internal Industrial and Business Trends', in *The Annals of the American Academy of Political and Social Science*, vol. 308, 1956.

'A Note on Capital-Output Ratio', in *Keizai Kenkyu*, vol. 7, n. 2, April 1956.

'Empirical Testing of the Macro-Economic Planning in Japan', in *Keizai Kenkyu*, vol. 9, n. 1, 1958.

Essays on Japanese Economy, Tokyo: Kinokuniya Co., Ltd., 1958.

Has Capitalism Changed?, edited by Shigeto Tsuru, Tokyo: Iwanami Shoten, 1961.

'Growth and Stability of the Post-War Japanese Economy', in *The American Economic Review*, vol. 51, n. 2, 1961.

'Post-War Democratization in Japan – Economics', in *International Social Science Journal*, 1961.

'The Applicability and Limitations of Economic Development Theory', in *The Indian Economic Journal*, vol. 9, n. 4, April 1962.

'Formal Planning Divorced from Action: Japan', in *Planning Economic Development*, edited by E. E. Hagen and Richard D. Irwin, Richard D. Irwin, Inc., Homewood, Illinois, 1963, pp. 119-149.

'Japanese Images of America', in *Paths of American Thought*, edited by Arthur M. Schlesinger, Jr., and Morton White, Boston: Houghton Mifflin Co., 1963, pp. 515-530.

'The Take-Off in Japan, 1868-1900', originally presented at the International Economic Association Meeting, Konstanz, September 1960; published in *The Economics of Take-Off into Sustained Growth*, edited by W. W. Rostow, London: Macmillan, 1963, pp. 139-150.

'The Economic Problems of Japan: Present and Future' and 'The Future of Japan in the Modern World – Including Relations With the United States and China', originally read as Dyason Memorial Lectures in Australia, October 1964; published in *The Australian Outlook*, 1964.

'Merits and Demerits of the Mixed Economy in Economic Development: Lessons from India's Experience', in *Studies on Developing Countries: Planning and Economic Development*, Warsaw: Polish Scientific Publishers, 1964.

'Survey of Economic Research in Postwar Japan – Major Issues of Theory and Public Policy Arising Out of Postwar Economic Problems', in *The American Economic Review*, vol. 65, n. 4, 1964, pp. 79-101.

'The Effects of Technology on Productivity', in *Problems in Economic Development*, edited by Edward A. G. Robinson, London: Macmillan, 1966, pp. 295-306.

Essays on Economic Development, Tokyo: Kinokuniya Co., Ltd., 1968.

'Marx and the Analysis of Capitalism: A New Stage on the Basic Contradiction?', originally presented at the Symposium on the Role of Karl Marx in the Development of Contemporary Scientific Thought, organized by UNESCO, May 1968; published in *Marx and Scientific Thought*, The Hague-Paris, Mouton, 1969, pp. 322-330.

'Environmental Pollution Control in Japan', originally presented at the Symposium on Environmental Disruption, organized by the International Social Science Council, Tokyo, March 1970; published in *Keizai Kenkyu*, vol. 21, n. 1, 1970.

'In Place of GNP', originally presented at the Symposium of Political Economy of Environment, organized by Maison des Sciences de l'Homme, July 1971; published in *Social Science Information*, August 1971, vol. 10 n. 4, pp. 7-21.

'"North-South" Relations on Environment', originally presented at the Columbia-United Nations Conference on Economic Development and Environment, New York, April 1972.

'Current Environmental Problems in Japan' originally presented at the International Congress of Scientists on Human Environment, Tokyo, November 1975.

'Towards a New Political Economy', in *Economics in the Future: Towards a New Paradigm*, edited by Kurt Dopfer, London: Macmillan, 1976, pp. 106-115; reprinted, Tokyo: Kodansha Ltd., 1976.

The Mainsprings of Japanese Growth. A Turning Point?, Paris: Atlantic Institute for Internatioanl Affairs, 1976.

'Higher Education in Transition', in *Perspectives for the Future System of Higher Education*, Research Institute for Higher Education, Hiroshima University, 1977.

'Introduction', in *Growth and Resource Problems Related to Japan*, edited by Shigeto Tsuru, The International Economic Association, Asahi Evening News, 1978.

'Energy Policy and Environmental Considerations in Japan', in *Energy Policy – The Global Challenge*, edited by Peter N. Nemetz, Journal of Business Administration, vol. 10, nos. 1 & 2, Canada: The University of British Columbia, Fall 1978/Spring 1979.

'Whither Japan? A Positive Program of Nation-Building in an Age of Uncertainty', in *Japan Quarterly*, vol. 27, n. 4, Oct.-Dec. 1980.

'The Significance of Marxian Political Economy in the Present-Day World', in *Classical Marxian Political Economy: Essays in Honor of*

184

Ronald L. Meek, edited by Ian Bradley and Michael Howard, London: Macmillan, 1982, pp. 276-290.

'A Peripatetic Economist', in *Banca Nazionale del Lavoro Quarterly Review*, n. 142, September 1982, pp. 227-244.

'A Survey of Economic Research in Japan, 1960-1983', in *Keizai Kenkyu*, vol. 35, n. 4, October 1984.

'History of Pollution Control Policy', in *Environmental Policy in Japan*, edited by Shigeto Tsuru and Helmut Weidner, Edition Sigma, Berlin, 1989.

'Keynote Address: Economics of Institutions or Institutional Economics', in *Economic Institutions in a Dynamic Society*, edited by Takashi Shiraishi and Shigeto Tsuru, London: Macmillan, 1989, pp. 1-23.

'Political Economy of Disarmament', in *Kokusaigakukenkyu*, March 1989.

'Political Economy of Urban Land – The Right of Property and "Price Revolution"', in *Unconventional Wisdom – Essays in Honor of John Kenneth Galbraith*, Boston: Houghton Mifflin Co., 1989.

'My Life Philosophy', in *The Life Philosophy of Eminent Economists*, edited by Michael Szenberg, Cambridge University Press, 1990.

2. *Books (in Japanese)*

National Income and Reproduction, 1946; *Inflation in Postwar Japan*, 1949; *Introduction to Economics*, 1954; *Logic and Reality in Economics*, 1959; *Giants in Modern Economic Sciences*, 1964; *Income and Welfare*, 1970; *Political Economy of Environmental Disruption*, 1972.

3. *Collected Works*

Collected Works, Tokyo: Kodansha, 1976, contains 13 volumes of Tsuru's work. Volumes 1 to 12 are in Japanese, while volume 13 is in English.

REFERENCES

AFL-CIO, *Automation and Technological Change*, 1958.

ALCHIAN ARMEN and HAROLD DEMSETZ, 'Production, Information Costs, and Economic Organization', *American Economic Review*, 62, 1972, pp. 777-796.

ARROW KENNETH, *Social Choice and Individual Values*, New York: John Wiley and Sons, 1963.

ATKINSON ANTHONY, *The Economics of Inequality*, Oxford: Clarendon Press, 1975.

BAUER OTTO, 'Die Akkumulation des Kapitals', *Die Neue Zeit*, vol. 31, n. 1, 1913.

BEVERIDGE WILLIAM H., *Full Employment in a Free Society*, London: George Allen and Unwin Ltd., 1944.

BLAUG MARK, *The Methodology of Economics*, Cambridge: Cambridge University Press, 1980.

BOULDING KENNETH, 'Income or Welfare', *The Review of Economic Studies*, vol. 17, 1949-1950, pp. 77-86.

BOULDING KENNETH E., 'A New Look at Institutionalism', *American Economic Review*, *May* 1957, pp. 1-12.

BUCHANAN JAMES M. and GORDON TULLOCK, *The Calculus of Consent*, Ann Arbor: University of Michigan Press, 1962.

CARVER THOMAS-NIXON, *The Distribution of Wealth*, New York, London: Macmillan, 1904.

CLAPHMAN JOHN, 'On Empty Economic Boxes', *Economic Journal*, vol. 32, 1922, pp. 305-314.

CLARK JOHN MAURICE, 'Memorial Address', in *Wesley Clair Mitchell – The Economic Scientist*, edited by ARTHUR F. BURNS, New York: National Bureau of Economic Research, 1952, pp. 139-143.

CLARK JOHN MAURICE, *Economic Institutions and Human Welfare*, 1st edition, New York: Knopf, 1957.

DOMAR ERSEY D. 'Expansion and Employment', *American Economic Review*, March 1947, pp. 34-55.

DORFMAN JOSEPH, *Thorstein Veblen and His America*, New York: The Viking Press, 1934.

DOWNS ANTHONY, *An Economic Theory of Democracy*, New York: Harper and Row, 1957.

DUESENBERRY JAMES S., *Income, Saving, and the Theory of Consumer Behavior*, first published as Harvard Economic Study, n. 87, Cambridge, Mass.: Harvard University Press, 1949; reprinted as a Galaxy Book, New York: Oxford University Press, 1967.

FISHER IRVING, 'What is Capital', *Economic Journal*, December 1896.

FISHER IRVING, *The Nature of Capital and Income*, New York; London: Macmillan, 1906.

FISHER IRVING N., *My Father Irving Fisher*, New York: Comet Press, 1956.

FREY BRUNO S., 'Politico-Economic Models and Cycles', *Journal of Public Economics*, vol. 9, 1978, pp. 203-220.

FRIEDMAN MILTON, 'The Economic Theorist', in *Wesley Clair Mitchell – The Economic Scientist*, edited by ARTHUR F. BURNS, New York: National Bureau of Economic Research, 1952, pp. 237-282.

FUJINO SHOZABURO, *Nihon Keizai Shimbun*, June 22, 1982.

GALBRAITH JOHN KENNETH, *American Capitalism: The Concept of Countervailing Power*, Boston: Houghton Mifflin, 1952.

GALBRAITH JOHN KENNETH, *The Affluent Society*, Boston: Houghton Mifflin, 1958.

GALBRAITH JOHN KENNETH, *The New Industrial State*, Boston: Houghton Mifflin, 1967.

GALBRAITH JOHN KENNETH, *The Age of Uncertainty*, Boston: Houghton Mifflin, 1977.

GALBRAITH JOHN KENNETH, *The Nature of Mass Poverty*, Cambridge, Mass.: Harvard University Press, 1979.

GALBRAITH JOHN KENNETH, *A Life in our Times*, London: André Deutsch Ltd., 1981.

GALBRAITH JOHN KENNETH, *Economics in Perspective: A Critical History*, Boston: Houghton Mifflin, 1987.

GROSSMANN HENRYK, *Das Akkumulations: und Zusammen-bruchsgesetz des kapitalistischen Systems*, Leipzig: C. L. Hirschfeld, 1929.

GRUCHY ALLAN G., 'Institutional Economics: Its Development and Prospects', in ROLF STEPPACHER, BRIGITTE ZOGG-WALZ, and HERMAN HATZFELDT, *Economics in Institutional Perspective: Memorial Essays in Honor of K. William Kapp*, Lexington, Mass.: Lexington Books D. C. Heath and Co., 1977, pp. 11-28.

REFERENCES

HANSEN ALVIN HARVEY, *Fiscal Policies and Business Cycles*, New York: W.W. Norton and Co., 1941.

HARROD ROY F., *The Trade Cycle: An Essay*, Oxford: Clarendon Press, 1936.

HARROD ROY F., *Towards a Dynamic Economics*, London: Macmillan, 1948.

HARROD ROY FORBES, *The Life of John Maynard Keynes*, London: Macmillan, 1951.

HOMAN PAUL T., 'Place in Contemporary Economic Thought' in *Wesley Clair Mitchell – The Economic Scientist*, edited by ARTHUR F. BURNS, New York: National Bureau of Economic Research, 1952, pp. 155-192.

JOHANSEN LEIF, 'A Method of Seperating the Effects of Capital Accumulation and Shifts in Production Function Upon Growth in Labour Productivity', *The Economic Journal*, December 1961, pp. 775-782.

KALDOR NICHOLAS, *An Expenditure Tax*, London: G. Allen and Unwin Ltd., 1955.

KAPP K. WILLIAM *Planwirtschaft und Aussenhandel*, Geneva: Geory et Cie, S.A. Librairie de l'Université, 1936.

KAPP K. WILLIAM *Towards a Science of Man in Society*, The Hague: M. Nijlioff, 1961.

KAPP K. WILLIAM, 'The Open-System Character of the Economy and Its Implications', in *Economics in the Future: Towards a New Paradigm*, edited by KURT DOPFER, London: Macmillan, 1976, pp. 90-105.

KENNEDY CHARLES, 'Technical Progress and Investment', *The Economic Journal*, June 1961, pp. 292-299.

KERR CLARK, *The Future of Industrial Societies: Convergence or Continuing Diversity?*, Cambridge, Mass.; London: Harvard University Press, 1983.

KEYNES JOHN MAYNARD, *The General Theory of Employment, Interest and Money*, London: Macmillan, 1936.

KEYNES JOHN MAYNARD, 'Economic Possibilities For Our Grandchildren', in *Essays in Persuasion*, London: Rubert Hart-Davis, Ltd., 1952, pp. 358-373.

KUTTNER ROBERT, 'The Poverty of Economics', *The Atlantic Monthly*, February 1985.

LANGE OSKAR, 'Marxian Economics and Modern Economic Theory', *Review of Economic Studies*, June 1935, pp. 189-201.

LEONTIEF WASSILY, 'The Significance of Marxian Economics for Present-Day Economic Theory', *American Economic Review*, Supplement, March 1938, pp. 1-9.

LERNER ABBA P., 'Saving Equals Investment', *Quarterly Journal of Economics*, February 1938, pp. 297-309.

LITTLE IAN M. D. and JAMES A. MIRRLEES, *Project Appraisal and Planning for Developing Countries*, London: Heinemann, 1974.

MANES PIETRO, *Critica del pensiero economico di Marx*, Bari: Dedalo, 1982.

MARCUSE HERBERT, *One Dimensional Man*, London: Routledge and Kegan Paul Ltd., 1964.

MARX KARL, *Capital*, vols. I, II, III, Chicago: Charles H. Kerr and Co. [c. 1909] – 1921.

MARX KARL, *Capital*, vol. I, translated from the fourth German edition by EDEN AND CEDAR PAUL, London: Allen and Unwin Ltd., 1928.

MARX KARL, *Capital*, vol. I, translated from the third German edition by SAMUEL MOORE and EDWARD AVELING and edited by FREDERICK ENGELS. A photographic reprint of the stereotyped edition of 1889, with supplement including changes made by Engels in the fourth German edition, with notes, Marx's preface to the French edition, notes on the English edition. Edited and translated by DONA TORR, London: Allen and Unwin Ltd., 1938 (1943).

MARX KARL, *Grundisse der Kritik der Politischen Ökonomie*, Berlin: Dietz Verlag, 1953.

MARX KARL, *Capital*, vols. I, II, III, Moscow: Foreign Language Publishing House, 1954-1962.

MARX KARL, *Theories of Surplus Value*, Moscow: Foreign Language Publishing House, vol. I, 1964.

MARX KARL, *Letters on 'Capital'*, translated by ANDREW DRUMMOND, London: New Park Publications Ltd., 1983.

MILL JOHN STUART, *Principles of Political Economy*, W. J. ASHLEY, ed., London: Longmans Green and Co., 1926.

MILLS FREDERICK C., 'A Professional Sketch' in *Wesley Clair Mitchell – The Economic Scientist*, edited by ARTHUR F. BURNS, New York: National Bureau of Economic Research, 1952, pp. 107-124.

MITCHELL WESLEY, *Business Cycles. The Problem and Its Setting*, New York: National Bureau of Economic Research, 1927.

MITCHELL WESLEY C., 'Institutes for Research in the Social Sciences', paper presented at the annual conference of the Association of American Universities, Chicago: University of Chicago Press, 1929.

MYRDAL GUNNAR, *The Political Element in the Development of Economic Theory*, translated by PAUL STREETEN, London: Routledge and Kegan Paul Ltd., 1953.

MYRDAL GUNNAR, 'Response to Introduction', *The American Economic Review*, May 1972, pp. 456-462.

MYRDAL GUNNAR, 'The Meaning and Validity of Institutional Economics', *Economics in the Future: Towards a New Paradigm*, ed. by KURT DOPFER, London: Macmillan, 1976, pp. 82-89.

MYRDAL GUNNAR, 'Institutional Economics', a lecture at the University of Wisconsin, December 15, 1977, reprinted in GUNNAR MYRDAL, *Essays and Lectures After 1975*, Kyoto: Keibunsha, 1979.

New Republic, July 29, 1940.

The New York Times, 'Booming Burglar Alarm Industry Finds That Fear of Crime Pays', August 16, 1970.

New York Times Magazine, December 18, 1966.

NISKANEN WILLIAM, *Bureaucracy and Representative Government*, Chicago: Aldine, Atherton, 1971.

OLSON MANCUR, *The Logic of Collective Action*, Cambridge, Mass.: Harvard University Press, 1965.

PIGOU ARTHUR C., *The Economics of Welfare*, London: Macmillan, 1932.

RIDKER RONALD G. and JOHN A. HENNING, 'The Determinants of Residential Property Values With Special Reference to Air Pollution', *The Review of Economics and Statistics*, May 1967, pp. 246-257.

RIESMAN DAVID, *Thorstein Veblen: A Critical Interpretation*, New York: Scribner's Sons, 1953.

ROBBINS LIONEL, *An Essay on the Nature and Significance of Economic Science*, London: Macmillan, 1935.

ROBINSON EDWARD AUSTIN G., ed., *Problems of Economic Development*, London: Macmillan, 1965.

ROBINSON JOAN, 'Introduction', in Rosa Luxemburg's *The Accumulation of Capital*, London: Routledge and Kegan Paul Ltd., 1951.

ROBINSON JOAN, 'The Production Function and the Theory of Capital – A Reply', *The Review of Economic Studies*, n. 62, 1955-1956, p. 247.

ROOSEVELT ELLIOT, ed., *The Roosevelt Letters*, vol. 3, London: George G. Harrap, 1949-1952.

ROUTH GUY and PETER WILES, eds., *Economics in Disarray*, Oxford: Basil Blackwell, 1984.

RUSKIN JOHN, *The Two Paths*, London: Smith and Elder, 1859.

SAMUELSON PAUL A., 'The Theory of Pump-Pricing Re-Examined', *American Economic Review*, September 1940, pp. 492-506.

SAMUELSON PAUL A., 'A Statistical Analysis of the Consumption Function', Appendix to ch. XI of ALVIN H. HANSEN, *Fiscal Policy and Business Cycles*, New York: Norton and Co., 1941, pp. 250-260.

SAMUELSON PAUL A., *Foundations of Economic Analysis*, 1st edition, Cambridge, Mass.: Harvard University Press, 1947.

SAMUELSON PAUL A., *Economics*, 11th edition, Tokyo: McGraw-Hill Kogakusha, 1979.

SAMUELSON PAUL A. and WILLIAM D. NORDHAUS, *Economics*, 12th edition, New York: McGraw-Hill, 1985.

SCHLESINGER ARTHUR M. JR. and MORTON WHITE, eds., *Paths of American Thought*, Boston: Houghton Mifflin, 1963.

SCHLESINGER ARTHUR JR., 'The Political Galbraith', *The Journal of Post-Keynesian Economics*, Fall 1984, pp. 7-17.

SCHUMPETER JOSEPH A., 'Über die mathematische Methode der Theoretischen Ökonomie', *Zeitschrift für Volkswirtschaft*, vol. 15, 1906.

SCHUMPETER JOSEPH A., *Business Cycles*, New York: McGraw-Hill, 1939.

SCHUMPETER JOSEPH A., *Capitalism, Socialism, and Democracy*, New York: Harper and Brothers, 1942.

SCHUMPETER JOSEPH A., *A History of Economic Analysis*, edited from manuscript by ELIZABETH BOODY SCHUMPETER, New York: Oxford University Press, 1954.

SCLOVE RICHARD, *The Bulletin of the Atomic Scientists*, May 1982, p. 44.

SEN AMARTYA K., 'The Impossibility of a Paretian Liberal', *Journal of Political Economy*, vol. 78, 1970, pp. 152-157.

SEN AMARTYA K., *An Economic Inequality*, Oxford: Clarendon Press, 1975.

SHIBATA KEI, *Theoretical Economics* (Riron Keizaigaku), Tokyo: Kobunsha, 1935, 1936.

SOLOW ROBERT M., 'Technical Change and the Aggregate Production Function', *The Review of Economics and Statistics*, August 1957, pp. 312-320.

STIGLER GEORGE J., 'Director's Law of Public Income Redistribution', *Journal of Law and Economic*, vol. 13, 1970, pp. 1-10.

SWEEZY PAUL M., *The Theory of Capitalist Development*, New York: Oxford University Press, 1942.

SWEEZY PAUL M., *The Present as History, Essays and Reviews on Capitalism and Socialism*, New York: Monthly Review Press, 1953.

SWEEZY PAUL M., 'Veblen on American Capitalism', in DOUGLAS F. DOWD ed., *Thorstein Veblen: A Critical Reappraisal*, Ithaca, N.Y.: Cornell University Press, 1958, pp. 177-197.

THUROW LESTER, *The Zero-Sum Society*, New York: Basic Books, 1980.

TINBERGEN JAN, *Selected Papers*, Amsterdam: North-Holland, 1959.

TSURU SHIGETO, 'On Reproduction Schemes', Appendix to PAUL M. SWEEZY, *The Theory of Capitalist Development*, New York: Oxford University Press, 1942.

TSURU SHIGETO, 'Marx's Theory of the Falling Tendency of the Rate of Profit', *The Economic Review*, July 1951, pp. 190-199.

TSURU SHIGETO, 'Marx's Tableau Economique and "Underconsumption' Theory', *Indian Economic Review*, February 1953, pp. 1-13.

TSURU SHIGETO, 'Merits and Demerits of the Mixed Economy in Economic Development: Lessons from India's Experiences', in *Studies on Developing Countries: Planning and Economic Development*, Warsaw: Polish Scientific Publishers, 1964.

TSURU SHIGETO, 'The Effects of Technology on Productivity', in *Problems in Economic Development*, edited by EDWARD A. G. ROBINSON, London: Macmillan, 1965.

TSURU SHIGETO, ed., *Proceedings of International Symposium on Environmental Disruption: A Challenge to Social Scientists*, Tokyo: International Social Science Council, 1970.

TSURU SHIGETO, 'In Place of GNP', originally at the Symposium on Political Economy of Environment, organized by Maison des Sciences de l'Homme, July, 1971, published in *Social Science Information*, 1971.

TUGWELL REXFORD G., *The Trend of Economics*, New York: A. A. Knopf, 1924.

TULLOCK GORDON, *The Politics of Bureaucracy*, Washington, D. C.: Public Affairs Press, 1965.

VARGA EVGENIJ, *World Economic Crisis*, 1, Moscow: State Social and Economic Press, 1937. (English title, but Russian text.)

VEBLEN THORSTEIN, *On the Nature of Peace*, New York: Macmillan, 1917.

VEBLEN THORSTEIN, *The Vested Interests and the State of the Industrial Arts*, New York: B. W. Huebsch, 1919.

VEBLEN THORSTEIN, *Absentee Ownership and Business Enterprise in Recent Times: The Case of America*, London: Allen and Unwin Ltd., 1924 [c. 1923].

VEBLEN THORSTEIN, *Essays in Our Changing Order*, ed. by LEON ARDZROONI, New York: The Viking Press, 1954 (1934).

VEBLEN THORSTEIN, *The Theory of Business Enterprise*, New York: Mentor Books, 1958 (1904).

The Wall Street Journal, July 23, 1970 'Lawyers Stand to Reap Substantial Rewards in Penn Central Case'.

WICKSELL KNUT, 1896, 'A New Principle of Just Taxation', in RICHARD A. MUSGRAVE and ALAN PEACOCK, eds., *Classics in the Theory of Public Finance*, New York, London: Macmillan, 1962, pp. 72-118.

WOLFE ALBERT B., 'Views on the Scope and Methods of Economics', in *Wesley Clair Mitchell – The Economic Scientist*, edited by ARTHUR F. BURNS, New York: National Bureau of Economic Research, 1952, pp. 207-234.

INDEX

INDEX

AFL-CIO 105
aggregates
  methodology of 17-39
  see also Keynesian aggregates; Marxian aggregates
Alexander, Sidney 175
Ardzrooni, Leon 59
Atkinson, Anthony 158
automation: Marx on 5-6, 120
Ayres, Clarence E. 71, 77

Bain, Joe 175
Baran, Paul 175
barter economy: Marx on 50
Bauer, Otto 28-9
behavioural hypotheses in institutional economics 149-50
Bergson, Abe 175
Böhm-Bawerk, E. von 18, 30
Boulding, Kenneth 96
Brinton, Crane 174
Bryce, Robert 175
Burke, Edmund 84
business
  in discussions 165
  Veblen on 61, 63
business cycles
  and capitalism 41-58
  and commodities 49-52
  contrasts between Schumpeter and Marx 56-8
  and credit creation 43-4, 46-7
  and crisis, possibility of 50, 83
  in discussions 162-3, 165-6
  and equilibrium 45-6, 48
  and innovation 43, 45
  in institutional economics 72
  Marx on 49-56
  Schumpeter on 41-9
  and surplus value 49-50, 52-3

Capital
  and social wealth 97
  as value concept 12-13
capitalism
  and business cycles 83; contrasts between Schumpeter and Marx 56-8;

Marx on 49-56; Schumpeter on 41-9, 56-8
  countervailing power to: Galbraith on 78
  and credit creation 43-4, 46-7
  and cybernetics 141-3
  and engineers: Veblen on 65
  and growth 102-3
  institutional economics differing from 103-7, 152-3
  and Keynesian aggregates 31-3, 36
  in Marxian aggregates 25-7, 29-30
  and Marx's tableau 9
  as mixed economy 102-3
  real and value aspects of 4-6
  and socialism in mixed economy 111-13
  state under: Veblen on 67-8
  and technology 107, 109, 112
  and value added 14
capitalist consumption, and Marx's tableau 10
Carver, Thomas-Nixon 163-4, 168
Cassel, G. 166
circular cumulative causation, in institutional economics 73, 101
Clapp, Gordon 174
Clark, John M. 71, 163-6, 168
class, in mixed economy 102-3
class struggle: Veblen on 69
Cobb-Douglas aggregate production function 11-12
collective action in economics, in discussions 158-9
collective choice in economics 81
  in discussions 149-50
commodities
  and business cycles 49-52
  in Keynesian aggregates 25
  in Marxian aggregates 26-7
Commons, John R, 71, 77, 163, 166, 168
constant capital, and Marx's tableau 9-10
consumer goods
  and aggregate analysis 18-20, 29-30
  and Marx's tableau 9-10

RAFFAELE MATTIOLI LECTURES

SCIENTIFIC COMMITTEE (May 1991): Sergio Steve, Chairman; Carlo Filippini, Mario Monti, Adalberto Predetti, Sergio Siglienti, Franco Venturi; Enrico Resti, Secretary.

ORGANIZATION: Banca Commerciale Italiana-Università Commerciale Luigi Bocconi · Milano.

ADMINISTRATION: Banca Commerciale Italiana · Milano.

PUBLISHER: Cambridge University Press · Cambridge.

RAFFAELE MATTIOLI FOUNDATION
Fondazione Raffaele Mattioli
per la Storia del Pensiero Economico

Published

RICHARD F. KAHN, *The Making of Keynes' General Theory* (First edition: May 1984; Japanese edition, Tokyo: Iwanami Shoten, Publishers, April 1987).

FRANCO MODIGLIANI, *The Debate over Stabilization Policy* (First edition: July 1986).

CHARLES P. KINDLEBERGER, *Economic Laws and Economic History* (First edition: December 1989; Italian edition, Bari: Laterza, 1990; Spanish edition, Barcelona: Editorial Crítica, December 1990).

ALAN PEACOCK, *Public Choice Analysis in Historical Perspective* (First edition: March 1992).

SHIGETO TSURU, *Institutional Economics Revisited* (First Edition: January 1993).

To be published

ERIK F. LUNDBERG, *The Development of Swedish and Keynesian Macro-economic Theory and its Impact on Economic Policy.*

NICHOLAS KALDOR, *Causes of Growth and Stagnation in the World Economy.*

RICHARD STONE, *Some British Empiricists in the Social Sciences.*

KARL BRUNNER - ALLAN H. MELTZER, *Money and the Economy. Issues in Monetary Analysis.*

PAUL PATRICK STREETEN, *Thinking About Development.*

DESIGN, MONOTYPE COMPOSITION AND PRINTING
BY STAMPERIA VALDONEGA, VERONA
JANUARY MCMXCIII